Uncle John's BATHROOM PUZZLER

BLOX

Bathroom
Ashland, Oregon

UNCLE JOHN'S BATHROOM PUZZLER

BLOX

For information, write...
The Bathroom Readers' Institute
P.O. Box 1117, Ashland, OR 97520
www.bathroomreader.com
E-mail: mail@bathroomreader.com

ISBN-13: 978-1-60710-563-3
ISBN-10: 1-60710-563-2

Printed in the United States of America
First printing: November 2012

1 2 3 4 5   16 15 14 13 12

Thank You!

The Bathroom Readers' Institute sincerely thanks the following people whose advice, assistance, and hard work made this book possible.

Gordon Javna

JoAnn Padgett

Melinda Allman

Stephanie Spadaccini

Lidija Tomas

Amy Goldstein

Mike Shenk

Robert Leighton

Derek Fairbridge

Jay Newman

Lorraine Bodger

Monica Maestas

Aaron Guzman

Rob Davis

Ginger Winters

Jennifer Frederick

Annie Lam

Lilian Nordland

Sydney Stanley

Brian, Trina, and Kim

Alfred Einstein

Felix the Wonder Dog

Sophie and JJ

Thomas Crapper

INTRODUCTION

Welcome to BLOX, the connect-the-letters word game that will keep your mind on the move for hours. The concept is simple: We'll provide you with a configuration of letters and tell you how many words we found. Your job is to find those words and scribble them down in the blanks. It's as simple as that.

As usual, we've got something for everyone, from easy (like the Basic BLOX puzzles) to "Einstein" (the diabolically difficult 3-Ds). The puzzles get harder as you work your way through the book, so even if you're a beginner, you could be a word puzzle expert by the time you're done.

Plus, our word-science staff here at the Bathroom Readers' Institute has hooked itself up to a dictionary that includes both common and uncommon words. That has made it possible for us to tell you exactly how many of each we found in each puzzle.

Keep in mind, too, that every section has its own distinct rules that differ a little from the general rules. Speaking of which...

HOW TO PLAY WITH BLOX

• Find as many words as you can by linking adjacent letters, moving horizontally, vertically, and/or diagonally.

• Use each letter only once to form a word. In other words, if there's just one O in a puzzle, you can't go back to that O to form MOJO or BOZO or OBOE.

• You can count both singular and plural forms of the same word—for example, PIT and PITS. Ditto for verb forms: BEG, BEGS, BEGGED, and BEGGING are all okay.

• You can't count proper nouns unless the section calls for them (see the

CATEGORY BLOX section, for example). The same goes for abbreviations, acronyms, contractions, hyphenated words, and foreign words that don't appear in an English dictionary.

• The minimum number of letters in the words you're looking for will vary from section to section. But don't worry—we'll remind you on every puzzle page, just below each set of BLOX.

But above all, the most important rule is to enjoy playing with your BLOX! Happy puzzling!

—**Uncle John and the BRI staff**

BASIC BLOX

Here's a good place to start. The rules are simple:
Find as many words as you can by linking up
adjoining letters and writing those words in the
blanks provided. We're mixing things up a bit here: In the
first 21 BLOX in this section, we're looking for words that
are **four letters or more**. In the last two BLOX, we're looking
for words that are **five or more letters**. But don't worry—
we'll remind you.

We found 56 common words and 26 uncommon
words of **four or more letters**.

*There's a Scrabble board in one of
every three U.S. households.*

Answers on page 240.

Lily, a blind dog in the UK, has her own seeing-eye dog.

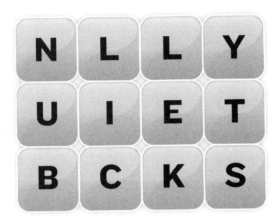

We found 74 common words and 30 uncommon words of **four or more letters**.

Between 1978 and 1980, Frenchman Michel Lotito ate an entire Cessna airplane.

Answers on page 240.

Total amount of money in a standard
Monopoly game: $15,140.

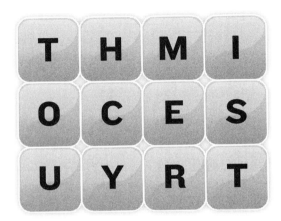

We found 42 common words and 23 uncommon
words of **four or more letters**.

Octopuses have rectangular pupils.

Answers on page 241.

Marie Osmond's actual first name: Olive.

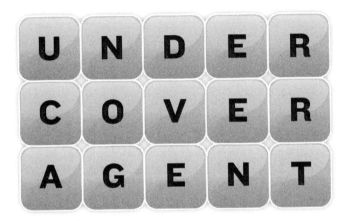

We found 70 common words and 33 uncommon
words of **four or more letters.**

*In 1951 parents could buy kids their own
"Atomic Energy Lab" for just $50...*

Answers on page 241.

*...The kit included actual
radioactive material.*

We found 63 common words and 34 uncommon words of four or more letters.

Pandas poop about 40 times a day.

Answers on page 241.

Monaco's philharmonic orchestra is larger than its army.

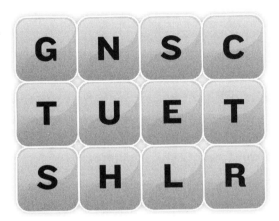

We found 82 common words and 28 uncommon
words of **four or more letters**.

*Q. What's the name of the patient in the game
Operation? A. Cavity Sam.*

Answers on page 242.

K2, Earth's second-highest mountain, kills one
climber for every four who summit.

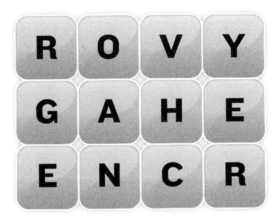

We found 66 common words and 17 uncommon words of four or more letters.

In Russian chess, the bishop is known as the "elephant."

Answers on page 243.

Anagram it: "Contradiction" becomes "accord not in it."

15

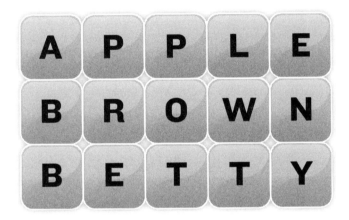

We found 52 common words and 24 uncommon
words of **four or more letters**.

*Q. Who designed Saddam Hussein's
bunker?...*

*...A. The grandson of the person who designed
Adolf Hitler's bunker.*

We found 69 common words and 39 uncommon
words of **four or more letters**.

Jimmy Carter had solar panels installed in the...

Answers on page 244.

...White House. Ronald Reagan had them removed.

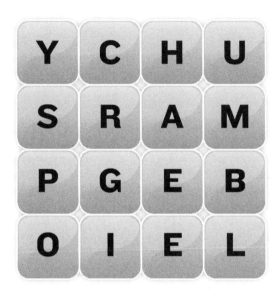

We found 138 common words and 65 uncommon
words of **four or more letters**.

The Chinese invented the fork.

Answers on page 244.

The USSR banned blind chess in 1930.

A	L	U	E
E	V	I	S
R	R	H	W
A	C	D	O

We found 95 common words and 43 uncommon
words of **four or more letters**.

An unprincipled but shrewd person is a "snollygoster."

Answers on page 245.

Asteroids can have their own moons.

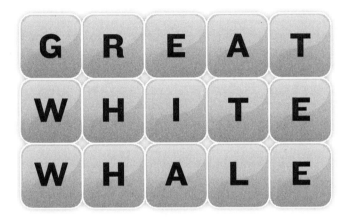

We found 59 common words and 21 uncommon words of **four or more letters**.

In 2011 Belgium set a record for the longest period without a federal government (250 days).

Answers on page 246.

"The billiard table is better than the doctor."
—Mark Twain

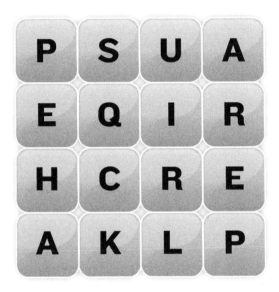

We found 64 common words and 32 uncommon
words of **four or more letters**.

*Price for an AK-47 gun in Kolowa, Kenya, in
1986: 15 cows. Price in 1996: 4 cows.*

Answers on page 246.

*February is the only month that can pass
without a single full moon.*

We found 57 common words and 27 uncommon
words of **four or more letters**.

Agent Orange wasn't orange—it was named for...

Answers on page 247.

...the orange stripe on the canisters that held the herbicide.

We found 101 common words and 33 uncommon
words of **four or more letters**.

*Brian May, guitarist for the band Queen,
has a PhD in astrophysics.*

Answers on page 247.

*Alter ego of Batman's puzzle-obsessed enemy
the Riddler: Edward Nygma.*

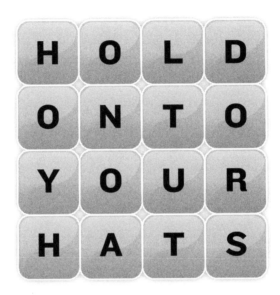

We found 71 common words and 26 uncommon
words of **four or more letters**.

Norway knighted a penguin in 2008—Sir Nils Olav.

Answers on page 248.

Some McDonald's salads contain more fat than Big Macs.

We found 48 common words and 32 uncommon
words of **four or more letters**.

The word "mafia" is never spoken in The Godfather.

Answers on page 249.

World's most shoplifted food: cheese.

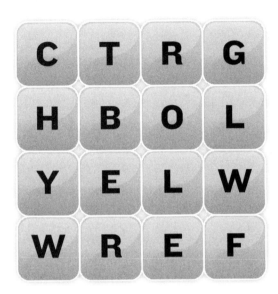

We found 97 common words and 43 uncommon
words of **four or more letters**.

*The 13 playing cards per suit represent
the lunar months in a year.*

Answers on page 249.

*The Earth gets 100 tons heavier every day—
thanks to falling space dust.*

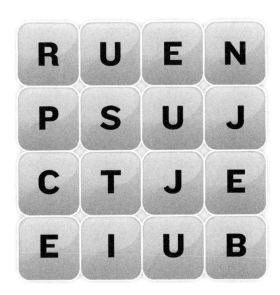

We found 30 common words and 12 uncommon
words of **four or more letters**.

*Q. What profession has the highest
suicide rate? A. Physicians.*

Answers on page 250.

*Dolphins name themselves with whistles and
keep those names throughout their lives.*

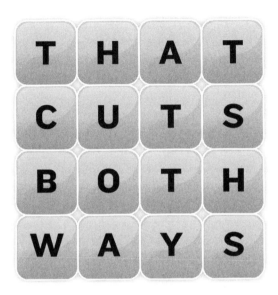

We found 74 common words and 29 uncommon
words of **four or more letters**.

The CIA once "recruited" a cat to spy on the Soviets...

Answers on page 250.

...but it was run over by a car.

We found 91 common words and 51 uncommon
words of **four or more letters**.

At Seattle's 1909 Alaska–Yukon–Pacific Exposition, a
month-old baby was...

Answers on page 251.

...given away in a raffle—and no one knows what happened to it.

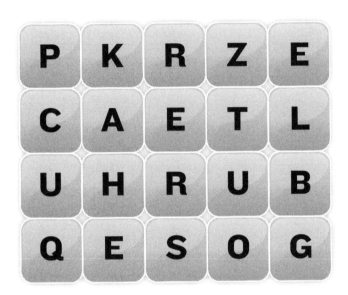

We found 125 common words and 54 uncommon
words of **five or more letters**.

Best-selling board game in the world: Monopoly.

Answers on page 252.

Afraid of wasps? You've got spheksophobia.

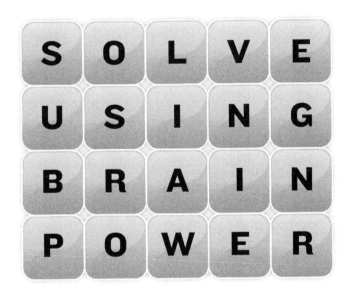

We found 101 common words and 66 uncommon
words of **five or more letters**.

Video game characters Mario and his brother
Luigi are known as...

Answers on page 253.

*...the "Mario Brothers"—making Mario's
last name Mario.*

MINI BLOX

O h, they're so cute! But that's not all. Our MINIs may be the smallest BLOX in the book, but each one is made up of a **nine-letter word**. So while you're looking for as many words as you can find of **three or more letters**, we hope you can also find the hidden treasure: the nine-letter word included in each 3 x 3 puzzle in this section.

The nine-letter word is

We found another 54 common words and 26 uncommon words of **three or more letters**.

Parcheesi is a corruption of the Hindi word pachis...

Answers on page 253.

...meaning "twenty-five," the game's highest roll.

The nine-letter word is

We found another 34 common words and 16
uncommon words of **three or more letters**.

*Author John Milton coined the word
"pandemonium" in* Paradise Lost.

Answers on page 254.

*Soviet premier Joseph Stalin sent his daughter's
first boyfriend to prison in Siberia.*

The nine-letter word is

We found another 35 common words and 24
uncommon words of **three or more letters**.

*Carl Sagan's favorite time-travel
movie:* Back to the Future Part II.

Answers on page 254.

Bowling balls were made out of wood until the early 1900s.

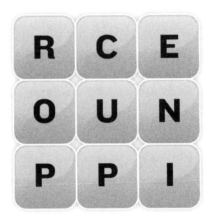

The nine-letter word is

_____

We found another 29 common words and II
uncommon words of **three or more letters**.

*Baby names rejected by New Zealand's department
of internal affairs: Anal, V8, and Lucifer.*

Answers on page 255.

*One of Jupiter's moons, Europa, contains more
than double the amount of water on Earth.*

The nine-letter word is

We found another 36 common words and 25 uncommon words of **three or more letters**.

Playing cards were introduced to Europe in the...

Answers on page 255.

...12th century by knights returning from the Near East.

The nine-letter word is

We found another 60 common words and 32
uncommon words of **three or more letters**.

In 1980, to honor his donations to a church in the city...

Answers on page 255.

...Saddam Hussein was given the key to Detroit.

The nine-letter word is

We found another 38 common words and 32 uncommon words of **three or more letters**.

There are 124 two-letter words allowed in Scrabble.

Answers on page 256.

The word "sudoku" is Japanese for "single number."

The nine-letter word is

_____

We found another 43 common words and 14 uncommon words of **three or more letters**.

U.S. president Rutherford B. Hayes's phone number: 1.

Answers on page 256.

In 1814 nine people were killed in the London Beer Flood.

The nine-letter word is

_____

We found another 64 common words and 32
uncommon words of **three or more letters**.

*There is no evidence that Viking warriors wore horned
helmets. Priests sometimes did, though.*

Answers on page 256.

*Actress Daryl Hannah is a cocreator of the
board game Liebrary.*

The nine-letter word is

_____

We found another 17 common words and 11
uncommon words of **three or more letters**.

*The first published crossword puzzle (1913)
used 32 words and...*

Answers on page 257.

*...was diamond shaped—there were
no black boxes in it.*

The nine-letter word is

We found another 19 common words and 12
uncommon words of **three or more letters**.

Olympic gold medals are made with 92.5 percent silver.

Answers on page 257.

Studies show: Cows orient themselves to magnetic north.

The nine-letter word is

We found another 25 common words and 15
uncommon words of **three or more letters.**

Most babies are born with blue eyes.

Answers on page 257.

Flamingo tongues were a delicacy in ancient Rome.

The nine-letter word is

We found another 56 common words and 27 uncommon words of **three or more letters**.

Name of the chesslike board game that C-3PO and Chewbacca play in Star Wars: Dejarik.

Answers on page 258.

In 1930 death row inmate William Kogut killed himself using a pipe bomb made of playing cards.

The nine-letter word is

_____

We found another 45 common words and 17
uncommon words of **three or more letters**.

The first slaves in North America were Irish...

Answers on page 258.

...prisoners sold by the British in the 1600s.

The nine-letter word is

We found another 84 common words and 39
uncommon words of **three or more letters**.

*The longest chess game lasted for 20 hours, 15 minutes
(269 moves)—it ended in a draw.*

Answers on page 258.

The fear of words is called "logophobia." The fear of long words: sesquipedalophobia.

The nine-letter word is

We found another 77 common words and 39
uncommon words of **three or more letters**.

*One form of brain damage causes sufferers
to want only gourmet food.*

Answers on page 259.

*Israeli army soldiers who admit to playing Dungeons
& Dragons are sent to military psychologists.*

The nine-letter word is

_____

We found another 47 common words and 23 uncommon words of **three or more letters**.

Nancy Reagan once dated Clark Gable.

Answers on page 260.

In the original Italian book, Pinocchio kills Jiminy Cricket.

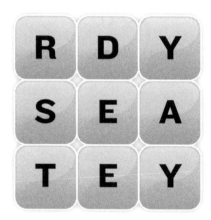

The nine-letter word is

_____

We found another 41 common words and 22
uncommon words of **three or more letters**.

*Twenty-seven million years ago in New Zealand,
penguins were almost 5 feet tall and 130 pounds.*

Answers on page 260.

"Playing bebop is like Scrabble with all the vowels missing." —Duke Ellington

The nine-letter word is

___

We found another 36 common words and 13
uncommon words of **three or more letters**.

Every year, Texas makes as much money as Russia.

Answers on page 261.

Jimmy Carter legalized home-brewed beer.

The nine-letter word is

We found another 32 common words and 7
uncommon words of **three or more letters**.

*The 1908 Olympics in London had the first opening
ceremony featuring national flags.*

Answers on page 261.

Monopoly has been published in 27 languages in more than 81 countries.

The nine-letter word is

_____

We found another 44 common words and 18
uncommon words of **three or more letters**.

Elephants are evolving without tusks because of poaching.

Answers on page 261.

Chutes and Ladders originated in 16th-century India.

The nine-letter word is

_____

We found another 36 common words and 31
uncommon words of **three or more letters**.

The longest vowel-only word playable in Scrabble: euouae…

Answers on page 261.

...It's a type of rhythm in music.

The nine-letter word is

_____

We found another 44 common words and 44
uncommon words of **three or more letters**.

Saturn's rings are only 30 feet thick.

Answers on page 262.

The UN has declared Internet access to be a basic human right.

CATEGORY BLOX

I n this section, your task is to find a certain number of words that belong in the given category. We'll tell you what the category is and how many answers there are. We'll even tell you how many common and uncommon words we found. Your answers—unless we say otherwise on the puzzle page—must be **at least three or more letters** (so, for example, don't count the OX you'll find in the MAMMALS puzzle as one of your words). But in each case, we'll identify the minimum number of letters you're looking for: words of three, four, five, or more letters.

Signs of the Zodiac

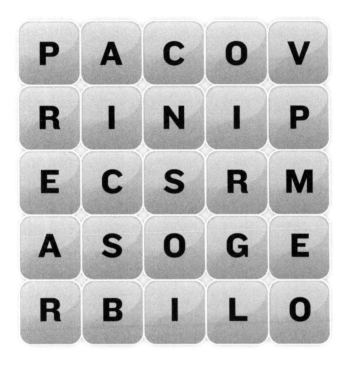

P	A	C	O	V
R	I	N	I	P
E	C	S	R	M
A	S	O	G	E
R	B	I	L	O

We found 9 signs of the zodiac with
three or more letters.

*Only English word with three consecutive
double letters: bookkeeper.*

_____

_____

_____

_____

_____

_____

_____

_____

_____

_____

_____

_____

_____

_____

_____

_____

_____

_____

_____

_____

_____

Answers on page 262.

In the book Goodnight Moon, *the time on the clocks changes from 7:00 p.m. to 8:10 p.m.*

Fruits

We found 11 common fruits and 1 uncommon one
with **four or more letters**.

Hippos kill more people every year than lions or crocodiles do.

Answers on page 262.

In 2008 J. K. Rowling made about $8 every second.

Parts of an Automobile

O	M	G	O	T
I	N	E	R	C
H	L	A	P	I
E	C	P	M	A
O	R	R	Y	A

We found 9 parts of an automobile with
four or more letters.

*Cornell University scientists created a functioning
guitar that was the size of a human blood cell.*

Answers on page 263.

*As a joke, a Manchester couple invited Queen
Elizabeth II to their 2012 wedding—she went.*

U.S. Presidents

D	A	N	T	M
M	A	G	A	U
S	B	E	R	F
Z	O	L	I	T
F	D	R	Y	A

We found 10 last names of U.S. presidents with
four or more letters.

A cat's hiss sounds like a snake on purpose.

Answers on page 263.

During WWII, some cars were converted to run on wood.

Mammals

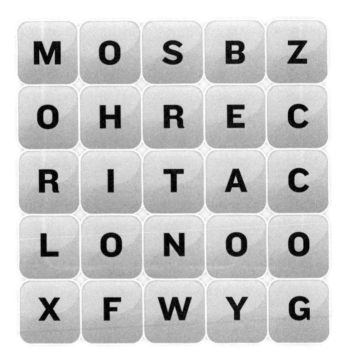

M	O	S	B	Z
R	H	R	E	C
R	I	T	A	C
L	O	N	O	O
X	F	W	Y	G

We found 14 common mammals and 1 uncommon one with **three or more letters**.

Q: Who was Nicholas Breakspear? A: The first and only Englishman to become pope.

Answers on page 263.

*From the starting position in chess, there are
eight ways to checkmate in two moves.*

Furniture

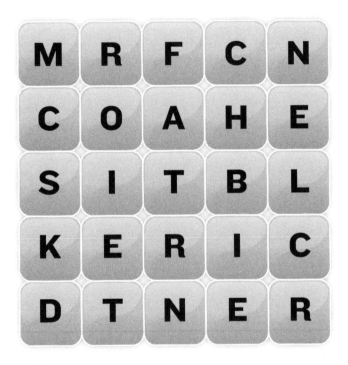

We found 12 furniture items with
three or more letters.

*Only major league baseball player to win a batting
title in three different decades: George Brett.*

Answers on page 263.

*On Neptune and Uranus, it
sometimes rains diamonds.*

Languages

P	S	E	K	H
G	E	O	T	S
S	R	A	N	I
I	M	A	D	L
A	N	S	P	O

We found 9 languages with **five or more letters**.

In the 1860s, prominent billiard players were so famous...

Answers on page 263.

...they were featured on trading cards.

Herbs and Spices

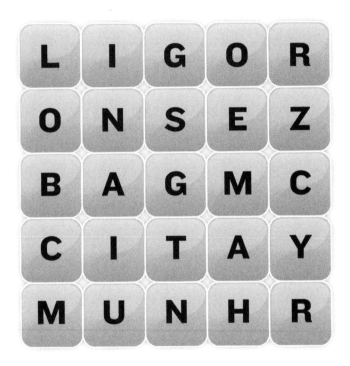

L	I	G	O	R
N	S	E	Z
O			
B	A	G	M	C
C	I	T	A	Y
M	U	N	H	R

We found 11 herbs and spices with
four or more letters.

First prize at the Wife Carrying World Championships...

Answers on page 263.

...in Sonkajärvi, Finland: the wife's weight in beer.

Shades of Red or Pink

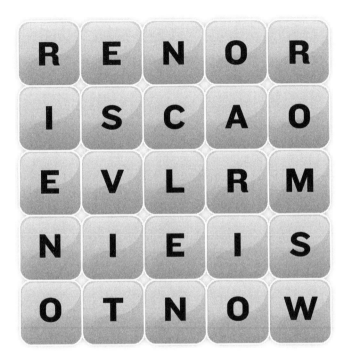

We found 9 shades of red or pink with
four or more letters.

*During the Civil War, Milton Bradley gave Union soldiers
board games small enough to fit into a knapsack.*

Answers on page 263.

*Human saliva contains a natural painkiller that
can be up to six times stronger than morphine.*

Summer Olympics Host Cities

We found 7 Summer Olympics host cities
with **five or more letters**.

*The 1908 Olympic Games featured
dueling—with wax bullets.*

Answers on page 263.

In Denmark, it's illegal to burn a foreign flag,
but legal to burn a Danish one.

Insects

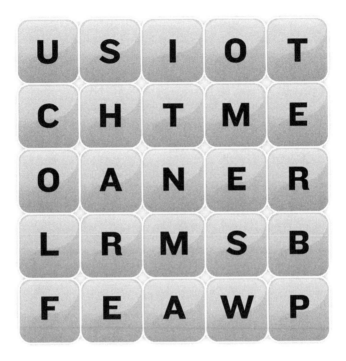

U	S	I	O	T
C	H	T	M	E
O	A	N	E	R
L	R	M	S	B
F	E	A	W	P

We found 10 insects with **three or more letters**.

Office cubicles were invented in 1968. Original name: the "Action Office System."

Answers on page 263.

*The small sleeve at the end of a pool
cue is called a "ferrule."*

Chemical Elements

We found 13 chemical elements with
three or more letters.

The most common answer in U.S. crossword puzzles: ERA.

Answers on page 263.

Anagram it: "Dormitory" becomes "dirty room."

Best Picture Winners

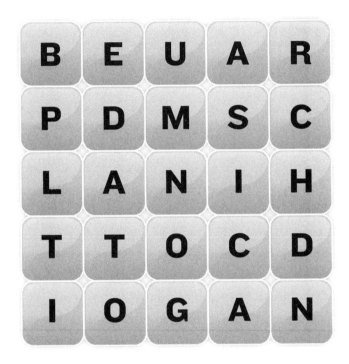

We found 7 Academy Award winners for Best
Picture with **five or more letters**.

Brazil once tried to sell an aircraft carrier on eBay.

Answers on page 263.

James Cagney never actually said, "You dirty rat."

Garden Vegetables

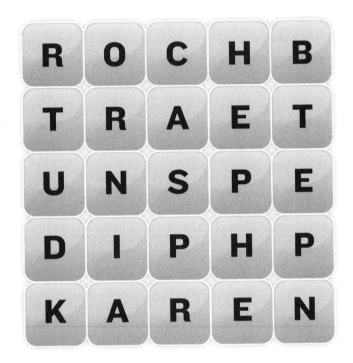

We found 10 garden vegetables with
four or more letters.

Current world record for solving a Rubik's Cube: 5.66 seconds.

Answers on page 263.

The first VCR was the size of an upright piano.

Musical Instruments

D	M	T	L	C
U	R	A	E	G
O	M	I	N	O
E	B	O	P	S
A	T	U	L	F

We found 13 common musical instruments and
3 uncommon ones with **four or more letters**.

Residents of Smithers, Canada, are known as Smithereens.

Answers on page 263.

Coyotes and badgers sometimes team up to hunt for food.

Bodies of Water

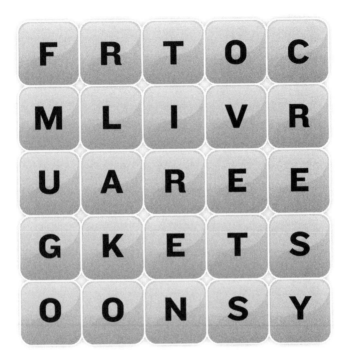

We found 10 common types of bodies of water
and 1 uncommon one with **three or more letters**.

*Mercury orbits the Sun faster than the
planet rotates on its own axis...*

Answers on page 263.

*...making one of Mercury's days
longer than one of its years.*

Countries of the World

We found 12 countries with **four or more letters**.

Nintendo was founded in 1889 as a playing card company.

Answers on page 264.

Cats don't have the taste buds that detect sweetness.

Flowers

D	I	P	C	O
S	E	H	A	R
O	N	D	L	X
D	R	I	L	O
M	A	A	G	Y

We found 9 common flowers and 1 uncommon
one with **four or more letters**.

New York Times *crossword editor Will Shortz holds a
degree in "enigmatology," the study of puzzles.*

Answers on page 264.

Sean Connery was offered the part of Gandalf
in the Lord of the Rings *trilogy. He declined.*

Hats and Headgear

We found 9 common types of hats and headgear
and 1 uncommon one with **five or more letters**.

*Youngest heavyweight boxing champ: Mike
Tyson, at 20 years, 4 months, 22 days.*

_____

_____

_____

_____

_____

_____

_____

_____

_____

_____

_____

_____

_____

_____

_____

_____

_____

_____

_____

_____

_____

_____

_____

Answers on page 264.

The phrases "straight and narrow," "feet of clay," and
"kiss of death" all originated in the Bible.

NBA Teams

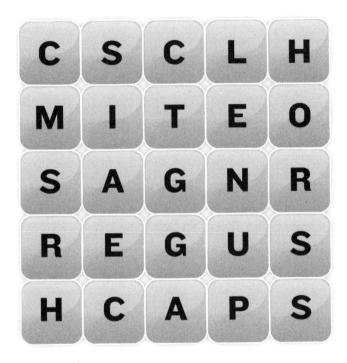

C	S	C	L	H
M	I	T	E	O
S	A	G	N	R
R	E	G	U	S
H	C	A	P	S

We found 9 NBA teams with **four or more letters**.

*Andrew Jackson was the only U.S. president
to pay off the national debt in full.*

Answers on page 264.

It takes more than 50 chemicals to
simulate the flavor of strawberry.

Fish

We found 8 fish with **four or more letters**.

Stomach acid is potent enough to dissolve razor blades.

Answers on page 264.

First American board game: The Mansion of Happiness (1843).

Dances

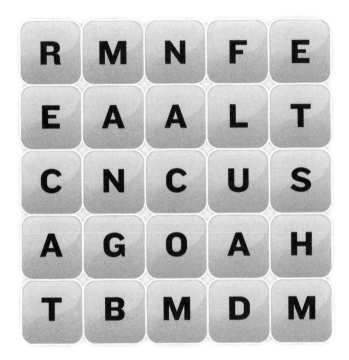

R	M	N	F	E
E	A	A	L	T
C	N	C	U	S
A	G	O	A	H
T	B	M	D	M

We found 9 common dances and I uncommon
one with **four or more letters**.

In 1950, at the Las Vegas Desert Inn, a
gambler had 27 straight wins...

Answers on page 264.

*...at craps. The odds of doing
that are 12,467,890 to 1.*

U.S. State Capitals

We found 8 U.S. state capitals
with **five or more letters**.

Chinese checkers was invented in Germany.

Answers on page 264.

Anagram it: "Snooze alarms" becomes "Alas, no more Zs."

SHAPELY BLOX

Oooh-la-la! On the following pages you'll find BLOX of unusual shapes and sizes to vex and perplex you. In this section, you'll be looking for as many words of **five or more letters** as you can find.

We found 98 common words and 61 uncommon
words of **five or more letters**.

The oldest known pair of dice—more than
4,000 years old—was found...

Answers on page 264.

...in Iran's "Burnt City," an archeological
site of Bronze Age artifacts.

We found 83 common words and 53 uncommon
words of **five or more letters**.

*Surgeons who grew up playing video games
make 37 percent fewer mistakes.*

Answers on page 265.

Total square miles of the Earth named for England's Queen Victoria: 1,188,100.

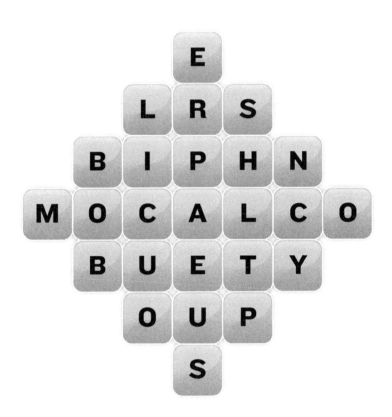

We found 81 common words and 58 uncommon
words of **five or more letters**.

*Film studio execs originally wanted O. J. Simpson
to the play the title role in* The Terminator...

Answers on page 266.

*...but director James Cameron
thought O. J. was "too nice."*

We found 39 common words and 46 uncommon
words of **five or more letters**.

Benjamin Franklin wrote an essay on farting.

Answers on page 266.

Chimps in Senegal hunt using wooden spears.

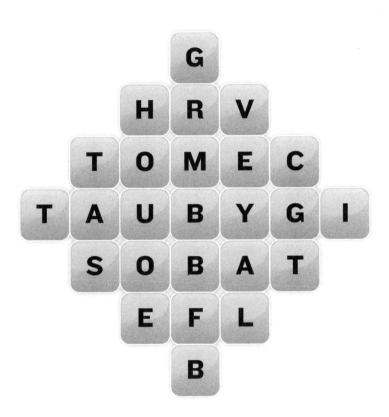

We found 72 common words and 55 uncommon
words of **five or more letters**.

A police detachment in British Columbia gives out...

Answers on page 267.

..."positive tickets" to exemplary citizens.

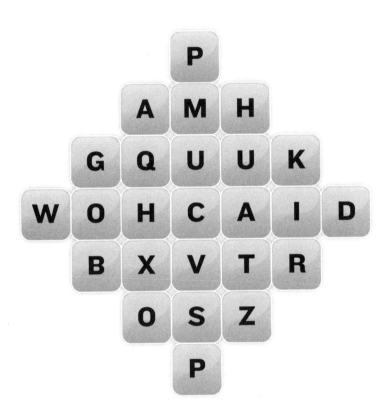

We found 26 common words and 15 uncommon
words of **five or more letters**.

*Studies show: Crows remember the faces of
humans who mistreat or threaten them.*

Answers on page 268.

*The Australian version of Monopoly includes
a pewter token in the shape of a koala.*

We found 23 common words and 15 uncommon
words of **five or more letters**.

Only U.S. president to write clues for a New
York Times *crossword puzzle: Bill Clinton.*

Answers on page 268.

Twenty percent of children between the ages of 11 and 13 hear voices in their heads.

We found 79 common words and 65 uncommon
words of **five or more letters**.

*PlayStation 3 game consoles were
used to study black holes.*

Answers on page 268.

*Richard Nixon used poker winnings to help
finance his first run for Congress.*

We found 134 common words and 79 uncommon
words of **five or more letters**.

*The last U.S. Civil War widow
died in 2003 at the age of 97...*

_____

_____

_____

_____

_____

_____

_____

_____

_____

_____

_____

_____

_____

_____

_____

_____

_____

_____

_____

_____

_____

Answers on page 269.

...She married her husband in 1924
when she was 18 and he was 81.

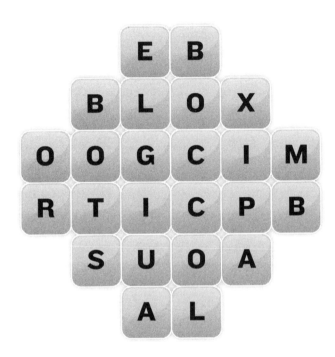

We found 47 common words and 37 uncommon
words of **five or more letters**.

*The act or practice of burying someone
alive is called "vivisepulture."*

Answers on page 270.

*"I failed to make the chess team because
of my height."* —Woody Allen

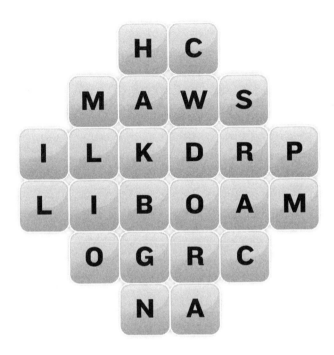

We found 74 common words and 34 uncommon words of **five or more letters**.

The first coin-operated pool table appeared in 1903. Cost: A penny.

Answers on page 270.

A historically insightful palindrome:
A man, a plan, a canal...Panama.

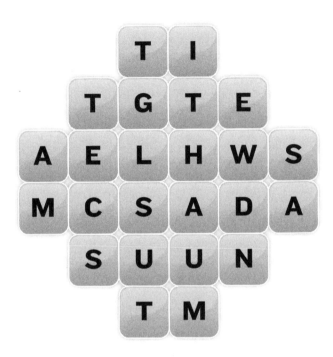

We found 90 common words and 55 uncommon
words of **five or more letters**.

*In 2006 a federal court judge in Florida settled
a dispute using the game of rock-paper-scissors.*

Answers on page 271.

*Abraham Lincoln suffered from depression and
never carried a knife, fearing he might kill himself.*

We found 88 common words and 60 uncommon
words of **five or more letters**.

*The largest known star (R136A1) is
265 times larger than our sun.*

Answers on page 272.

*In the U.S., doctors' sloppy handwriting on prescriptions
kills more than 7,000 people annually.*

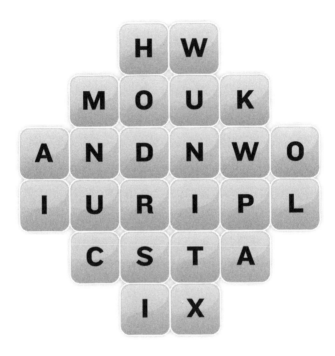

We found 61 common words and 51 uncommon
words of **five or more letters**.

The plane-launching mechanism on an aircraft carrier...

Answers on page 273.

...could throw a pickup truck more than a mile.

We found 68 common words and 37 uncommon
words of **five or more letters**.

*Tomb Raider's Lara Croft was
originally named Laura Cruz.*

Answers on page 273.

*The first jigsaw puzzle was created by
mapmaker John Spilsbury.*

We found 28 common words and 14 uncommon words of **five or more letters**.

Playing cards were invented in ancient China.

Answers on page 274.

The last McDonald's in Iceland closed in 2009.

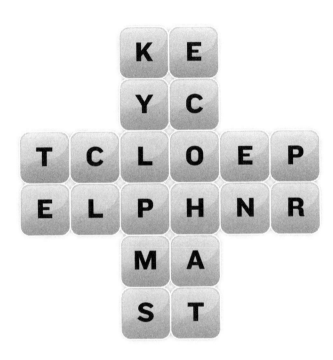

We found 31 common words and 10 uncommon
words of **five or more letters**.

*The ashes of Dr. Fredric J. Baur, the
deceased designer of the...*

Answers on page 274.

*...Pringles potato chip tube, were
buried in a potato chip tube.*

We found 95 common words and 52 uncommon
words of **five or more letters**.

*J. Edgar Hoover and Mao Tse-tung both
once worked as librarians.*

Answers on page 274.

*Got wavy hair? Then you
are "cymotrichous."*

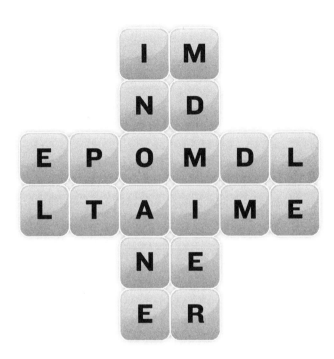

We found 44 common words and 41 uncommon
words of **five or more letters**.

*John Quincy Adams installed the first
pool table in the White House.*

Answers on page 275.

*There are 2,598,960 possible hands in
a five-card poker game.*

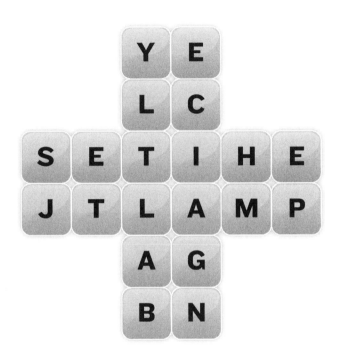

We found 83 common words and 46 uncommon
words of **five or more letters**.

Some fish can change gender.

Answers on page 276.

Fourth-century Chinese currency included knives.

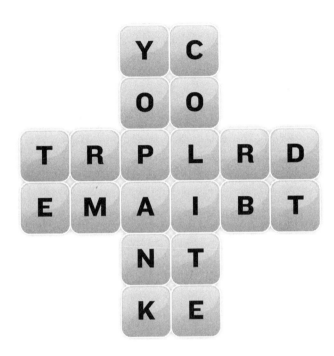

We found 81 common words and 58 uncommon
words of **five or more letters**.

*In South Korea, it's illegal for kids under 16 to play
video games after midnight.*

Answers on page 276.

*Scrabble inventor Alfred Butts once confessed
to being a terrible speller.*

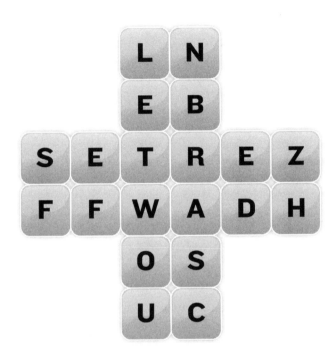

We found 71 common words and 31 uncommon
words of **five or more letters**.

The Lydians of Asia Minor invented cubical dice.

Answers on page 277.

Most common surname in China: Wang.

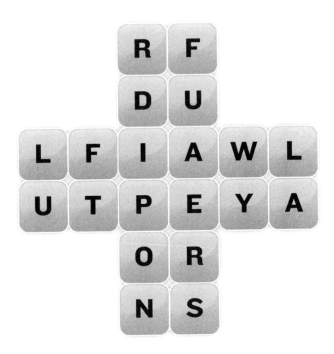

We found 44 common words and 14 uncommon words of **five or more letters**.

Q: Who were William Arden, Charles Barrow, and Ernest Hall? A: Shakespeare...

Answers on page 278.

*...Dickens, and Hemingway if they had taken
their mothers' maiden names.*

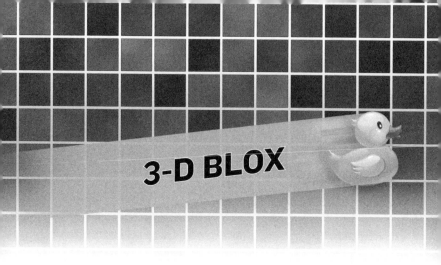

3-D BLOX

or experts only? Perhaps. We consider our 3-D BLOX the killer of the species. In this section, you're looking for **five-letter words** only. And in case you lose your way in the maze of letters, remember that the rule still holds: you can use each letter just once in each word.

We found 13 common words and 1 uncommon
word of **five letters only**.

The murder-mystery game Clue is called Cluedo in the UK...

Answers on page 278.

...a play on "clue" and "ludo" (Latin for "I play").

We found 14 common words and 3 uncommon
words of **five letters only**.

*"Daring ideas are like chessmen moved forward. They may
be beaten, but they may start a winning game." —Goethe*

Answers on page 278.

Longest English word that can be spelled out using musical notes: cabbaged.

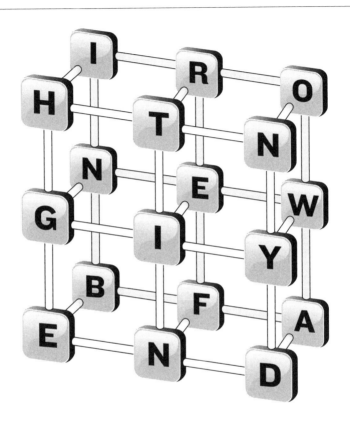

We found 20 common words and 4 uncommon
words of **five letters only**.

*First commercially sold, coin-operated
video game: Computer Space (1971).*

Answers on page 278.

The Great Pyramids weren't actually built by
slaves, but by skilled Egyptian laborers.

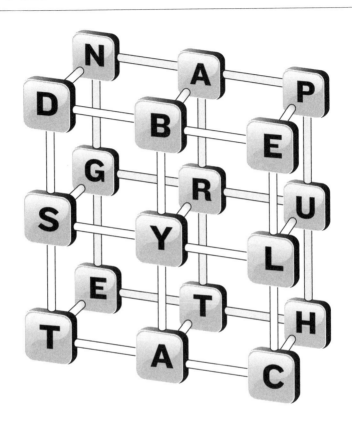

We found 18 common words and 1 uncommon
word of **five letters only**.

*NASA pays volunteers $15,000 to lie in bed for
90 days to monitor the effects of zero gravity.*

Answers on page 278.

J. R. R. Tolkien typed the entire Lord of the Rings *trilogy using two fingers.*

We found 17 common words and 5 uncommon
words of **five letters only**.

The queen of England does not have a passport.

Answers on page 279.

Joseph Stalin reportedly tried to have John Wayne killed.

3-D BLOX #6

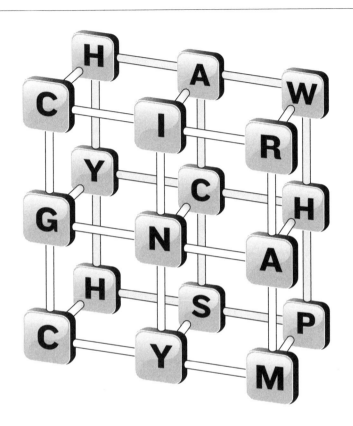

We found 17 common words and 6 uncommon
words of **five letters only**.

*Hatsune Miku, a Japanese virtual pop star,
gives concerts as a 3-D hologram.*

Answers on page 279.

*Bulletproof vests were invented in 1969 by a
pizza delivery guy in Detroit.*

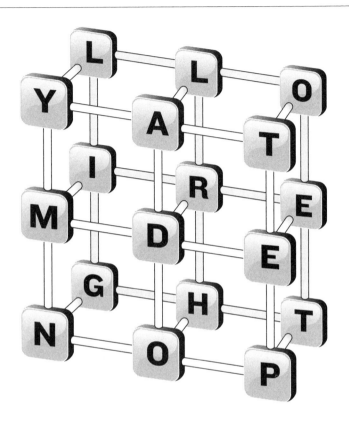

We found 18 common words and 2 uncommon
words of **five letters only**.

*From memory, autistic savant Daniel Tammet
recited pi to 22,514 digits.*

Answers on page 279.

*The first chessboard with alternating light and
dark squares appeared in Europe in 1090.*

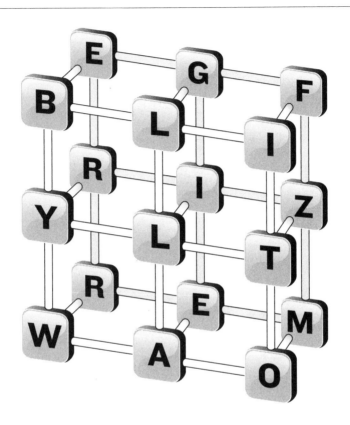

We found 11 common words and 1 uncommon
word of **five letters only**.

The best-selling mobile game of all time: Tetris.

Answers on page 279.

North Korea has a black market for candy.

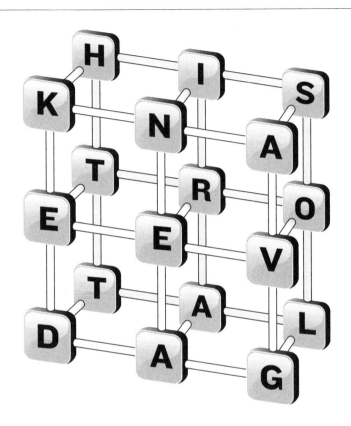

We found 25 common words and 10 uncommon
words of **five letters only**.

*During WWII, Japan dropped "bombs" of
plague-infected fleas on China.*

Answers on page 279.

*Placed end to end, all the Scrabble tiles ever produced
would reach around the Earth eight times.*

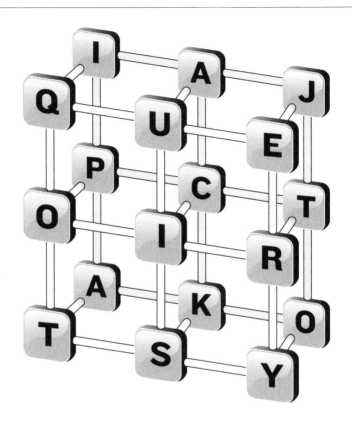

We found 8 common words and 5 uncommon
words of **five letters only**.

*Q: What do the board games Clue, Monopoly, and Battleship
have in common? A: All have been adapted as feature films.*

Answers on page 279.

*Until the 1400s, the queen in chess was called
the "fers," an adviser to the king.*

We found 16 common words and 6 uncommon
words of **five letters only**.

*The only coach in the history of University
of Kansas basketball to have a...*

Answers on page 279.

*...losing record was James Naismith,
the inventor of basketball.*

We found 30 common words and 8 uncommon
words of **five letters only**.

Monopoly property Marvin Gardens is a misspelling...

Answers on page 279.

...of a real Atlantic City location, Marven Gardens.

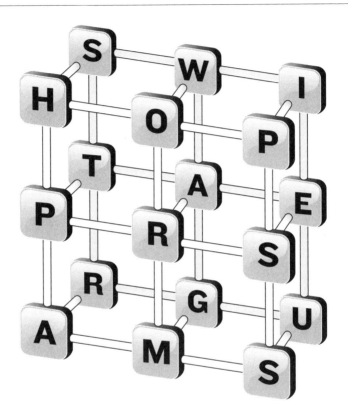

We found 22 common words and 3 uncommon words of **five letters only**.

Faulker, Hemingway, and Fitzgerald were all bad spellers.

Answers on page 280.

The Ebola virus is named for Zaire's Ebola River.

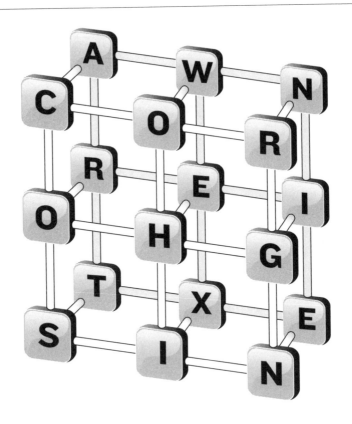

We found 20 common words and 3 uncommon words of **five letters only**.

The world's largest crossword puzzle, published in Russia, contained 64,371 words.

Answers on page 280.

In 1974 a collector's edition of Monopoly—with gold houses and silver hotels—sold for $25,000.

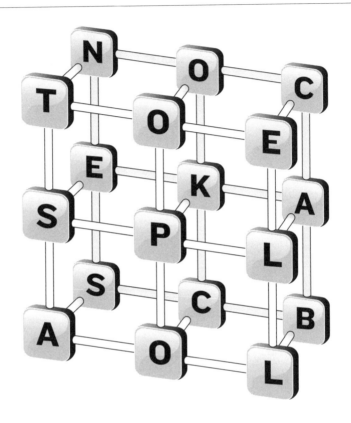

We found 18 common words and 3 uncommon
words of **five letters only**.

*"The game of chess is a lake in which a mosquito can bathe
and an elephant can drown." —Indian proverb*

Answers on page 280.

First film to feature a nude scene: Back to God's Country *(1919).*

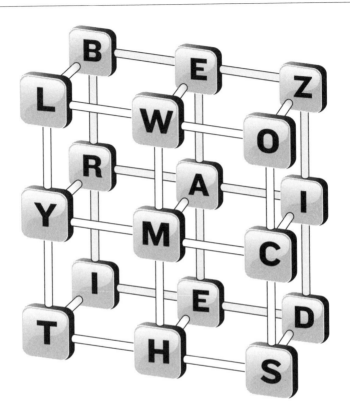

We found 13 common words and 2 uncommon
words of **five letters only**.

*Russia has the most chess grand masters
(186). Germany is second (73)...*

Answers on page 280.

*...The Ukraine is third (69), and the
United States fourth (65).*

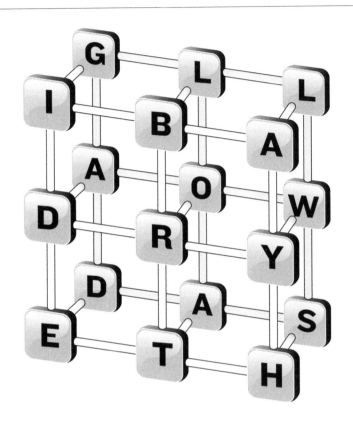

We found 23 common words and 2 uncommon
words of **five letters only**.

*In 2003 the U.S. army established a military
base on top of the site of ancient Babylon.*

Answers on page 280.

Q: How old was George S. Parker when he launched
the Parker Brothers' game company? A: 16.

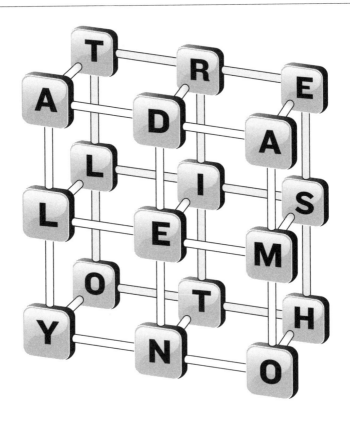

We found 24 common words and 5 uncommon words of **five letters only**.

Bermuda and the Turks and Caicos Islands have expressed interest in joining Canada.

Answers on page 280.

The lowest known note in the universe, emitted by a black hole, is 57 octaves below middle C.

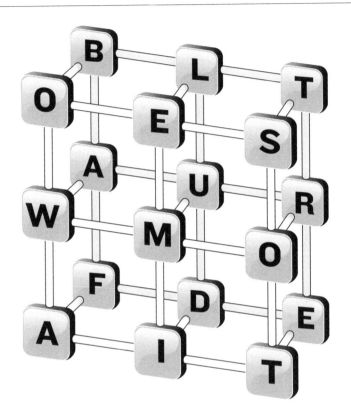

We found 21 common words and 10 uncommon
words of **five letters only**.

*Returning Apollo 11 astronauts had to declare
their moon rocks at U.S. customs.*

Answers on page 280.

English Scrabble has 100 tiles—Italian and Portuguese versions have 120.

We found 16 common words and 4 uncommon
words of **five letters only**.

*Q: What do the words "aceriflorum" and
"facetious" have in common?...*

Answers on page 281.

*... A: They both contain all
the vowels in order.*

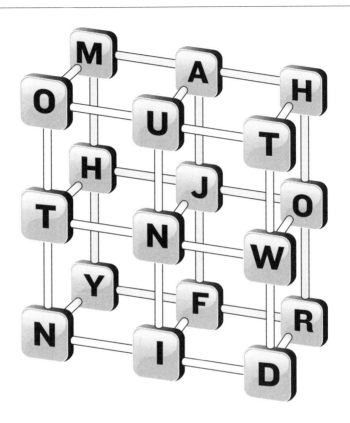

We found 12 common words and 2 uncommon words of **five letters only**.

Milton Bradley's original name for the game Twister: Pretzel.

Answers on page 281.

The jack of clubs in a deck of cards
represents Sir Lancelot.

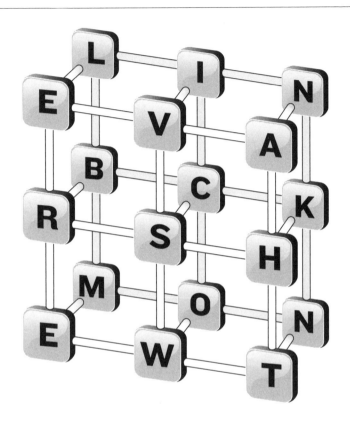

We found 18 common words and 5 uncommon
words of **five letters only.**

*The name of the pool "cue" is a corruption of the
Old French* queue, *meaning "tail."*

Answers on page 281.

Anagram it: "Eleven plus two" becomes "twelve plus one."

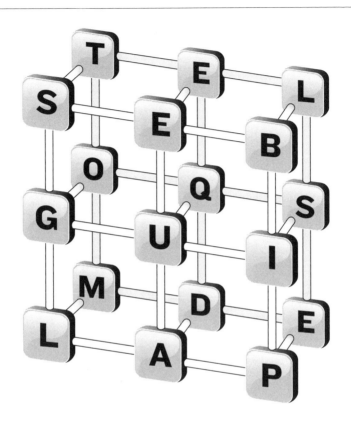

We found 18 common words and 4 uncommon
words of **five letters only**.

Fastest official completion of a New York Times
crossword puzzle: 2 minutes, 14 seconds.

Answers on page 281.

*Studies show: People can solve anagrams
faster while lying on their backs.*

ANSWERS

COMMON WORDS

CAMP
CAMPIER
CARE
CARET
CARP
CATER
CERIUM
GIMP
GRACE
GRAM
GRAMP
GRATE
GRAVY
GRAY
GREAT
GRIM
GRIMACE
GRIP
IRATE
MACE
MARE
MATE
MATER
MIGRATE
MIRE
PIER
PIETY
PIMA
PIRATE
PRAM
PRAT
PRATE
PRAY
PRIG
PRIM

PRIMA
PRIMATE
PRIVATE
PRIVY
PUMA
RACE
RAMIE
RAMP
RATE
REACT
REAM
TAMP
TARP
TEAM
TEAR
UMPIRE
UPRATE
VAMP
VAMPIER
VAMPIRE
VARIETY

UNCOMMON WORDS

AIGRET
AMIE
AMIR
CAMPI
CARPI
CATE
CAVIE
CAVY
CERIA
GRAT
IMARET
MACER
MAIGRE
MAIR
MAVIE

PIETA
PREACT
RAMI
RECTA
TACE
TARE
TERAI
UMIAC
VAIR
VIER
YARE

BASIC BLOX #2

COMMON WORDS

BIKE
BIKES
BILE
BILES
BILL
BILLET
BILLETS
BILLY
BUCK
BUCKET
BUCKETS
BUCKS
BUILT
BULL
BULLET
BULLETS
BULLIES
BULLIEST
BULLY
CELL
CELLI
CULL
ICES
ILLEST

ILLY
INLET
INLETS
KELLY
KILL
KILN
KILT
KILTS
LEST
LETS
LICE
LICK
LICKS
LIES
LIKE
LIKELY
LIKES
LILT
LILTS
LILY
LUCK
LUCKIEST
LUCKILY
LUCKS
LYES
NICE
NICELY
NICEST
NICETY
NICK
NICKEL
NICKS
NUBILE
NULL
SELL
SKEIN
SKELL

SKILL
SKILLET
SKIN
STEIN
STYE
STYLE
STYLI
TELL
TELLY
UNLET
UNLIKE
UNLIKELY
YELL

UNCOMMON WORDS

BICE
BICES
CEIL
CELT
CELTS
CULET
CULETS
CULLET
CULLETS
CULLIES
CULLY
KELT
KELTS
KILTY
LEKS
LIKEST
LUCE
LUCES
LUCKIE
LUCKIES
LUNIES
LUNIEST
NILL

NUCELLI
SKIEY
STELIC
STEY
TELIC
TYES
UBIETY

BASIC BLOX #3

CHEMIST
CHEMISTRY
CHEST
COYER
COYEST
CREST
ECHO
HEIST
HEMS
HERS
MERCY
MISER
MISERY
MIST
MISTER
OCHER
OCHERS
OHMS
OTHER
OTHERS
OUCH
OUCHES
RECTO
REST
RYES
SECT
SEMI
STEM

TECH
THEISM
THEIST
THEM
THEY
THOU
TOUCH
TOUCHE
TOUCHER
TOUCHERS
TOUCHES
TOYER
TOYERS
TREY

CHERT
CHERTS
ECHT
ERST
HEST
HETS
MERC
MERCH
MISE
OCHERY
OYER
OYERS
OYES
REIS
REMS
RETS
RYOT
STEY
TOCHER
TOCHERS
TRES
YECH

YUCH

BASIC BLOX #4

AGENT
CAGE
CODE
CODER
COGENT
CONVENE
CONVENED
CONVENER
CONVENT
CONVERT
CONVERTED
CONVERTER
COVE
COVEN
COVER
COVERED
COVERER
COVERT
COVET
DEER
DENT
DOGE
DOVE
ENTER
ENTERED
ENTERER
ENTREE
ERRED
EVEN
EVENED
EVENER
EVENT
EVER
EVERT

EVERTED
GEED
GENE
GENRE
GENT
GEODE
GOVERN
GOVERNED
NEED
NEON
NEVER
NODE
OVEN
OVER
OVERT
REDO
REED
RENT
RERENT
REVERT
TEED
TEEN
TERN
TREE
TREED
UNCAGE
UNCOVER
UNCOVERED
UNDER
UNDO
VEER
VEERED
VENEER
VENT
VENTED
VENTER

ACNODE
AGEE
AGENE
AGENTED
AGON
COAGENT
CODEN
CONVENTED
COVED
DEET
DENE
DERE
DEVON
DOVEN
ERNE
GENET
GODET
NEEDER
NEVE
OGEE
OVERED
REDE
REDON
REEVE
REEVED
REVET
TEREDO
TERNE
TREEN
UNCO
UNDE
UNDEE
VERT

BASIC BLOX #5

ABUT

ANSWERS

ANTE	MATE	ETAMIN	HENS	SHUNS
AUNT	MATER	ETNA	HUES	SHUNT
BAIL	MATURE	INIA	HUNG	SHUT
BALM	MAUL	INTURN	HUNS	SNUG
BANTER	MINI	INURN	HUNT	STENT
BATE	MINIATURE	LABRET	HUNTS	STENTS
BLAM	MINT	LATU	HUSTLE	STRENGTH
BLAT	MINTER	LIMAN	HUSTLER	STRENGTHS
BLINI	MINUET	LINTER	HUTS	STUN
BLUE	MINUTE	LUNATE	LENGTH	STUNG
BLUER	MINUTER	LUNT	LENGTHS	STUNS
BLUNT	NAIL	MAUN	LENS	SUER
BLUNTER	NATURE	MAUT	LENT	SUES
BLUR	RETAIL	MIAUL	LEST	SUET
BLURT	RETAIN	MINA	LETS	SUETS
BRUNT	RUNT	TABU	LUNG	SUNG
BRUT	TAIL	TABULI	LUSH	SUNS
BRUTAL	TERN	TABUN	LUSHER	SUNSET
BRUTE	TRUE	TAIN	LUSHES	TENS
BUNT	TUBA	TALI	LUSHEST	TENT
BUNTER	TUBAL	ULAN	LUST	TENTH
BURN	TUNA	UNAI	LUSTER	TENTHS
INTER	TURBAN	UNBAN	NERTS	TENTS
INTERN	TURN	BASIC BLOX #6	NEST	THEN
INURE	URBAN	COMMON WORDS	NETS	THUG
LAIN	UNCOMMON WORDS	CENSUS	NUTS	THUS
LANTERN	AMIN	CENT	REHUNG	TUNE
LATE	ANIL	CENTS	RENT	TUNER
LATER	ANTRE	GNUS	RENTS	TUNES
LIMA	BANI	GUEST	REST	TUSH
LINT	BLAIN	GUNS	RESULT	TUSHES
LUNA	BLATE	GUNSEL	SCENT	USER
LURE	BLIN	GUSH	SCENTS	USHER
LUTE	BLUET	GUSHER	SECT	UNCOMMON WORDS
MAIL	BUNA	GUSHES	SENT	CELT
MAIN	BURET	GUST	SHES	CELTS
MANURE	BUTE	GUTS	SHUN	CENTU

GULES
HENT
HENTS
HERL
HEST
HETS
LUES
LUNE
LUNES
LUNET
LUNETS
LUNT
LUNTS
LUSTRE
RECS
RETS
SHENT
SHUL
THENS
TRES
TULE
TULES
TUNG
TUNS
UNSET

BASIC BLOX #7

COMMON WORDS

ACHE
ACHY
ACNE
ACRE
ANCHOR
ANCHOVY
AVER
CAGE
CANE
CARGO

CAVE
CAVER
CHANGE
CHAR
CHARGE
EACH
EAVE
ECHO
ENGRAVE
ENGRAVER
GAVE
GEAR
GRACE
GRAN
GRAVE
GRAVER
GRAVY
GROAN
GROVE
HANG
HANGOVER
HAVE
HOAR
HOGAN
HORA
HOVE
HOVER
NACHO
NAVE
NAVY
NEAR
ORANG
ORANGE
ORGAN
OVER
OVERCHARGE
OVERHANG

RACE
RACER
RAGE
RANCH
RANCHER
RANCHO
RANG
RANGE
RAVE
RAVER
RECANE
RECHANGE
RECHARGE
REHANG
ROACH
ROAN
ROVE
ROVER
VANE

UNCOMMON WORDS

ANCHO
CAVY
CHANG
CHAO
CHEVY
GAEN
GANE
GNAR
HAEN
HANCE
HAVER
NACRE
ORACH
ORACHE
RANCE
VANG
YECH

BASIC BLOX #8

COMMON WORDS

ABET
ABETTOR
APORT
APPLE
BARB
BARE
BETTOR
BROW
BROWN
LENT
LENTO
LORE
NEWT
OTTER
PARE
PAROLE
PART
PLENTY
PLOP
PLOT
PLOTTER
PLOW
POET
POLE
PORE
PORT
POTTER
POTTY
PREOP
PRETTY
PROLE
PROP
PROW
PROWL
ROLE

ROTE
TOPPLE
TORE
TORT
TORTE
TOTE
TOTER
TOWEL
TOWN
TOWNY
TRAP
TROT
TROWEL
TWENTY
WENT
WORE
WORT

UNCOMMON WORDS

ABBE
AREOLE
BARBE
BARBET
BROWNY
LOTTE
LOTTER
LOWE
LOWN
PAREO
PAROL
PLEW
PLOTTY
POWTER
RABBET
ROTTE
ROWEL
ROWEN
TOLE

ANSWERS

TORA	MOLAR	ZEAL	TOEA	BLEARS
TOWY	MOLE	ZEALOT	TOLA	BLEARY
TROP	MONTE	UNCOMMON WORDS	TOLAR	CABER
TROW	MONTH	ARYL	TOLE	CABERS
TYNE	MONTHLY	ATOPY	TYPAL	CABLE
BASIC BLOX #9	MOPY	EATH	**BASIC BLOX #10**	CAGE
COMMON WORDS	MOTE	ETALON	COMMON WORDS	CAGER
AEON	MOTEL	HOLARD	ABLE	CAGERS
ALOE	MOTH	HOLM	ABLER	CAGIER
APTLY	NOEL	JALOP	ACRE	CAME
ATOM	NOTARY	JATO	AGREE	CAMEL
ATOP	NOTE	JEON	AMBER	CARE
DRAT	OATH	JEOPARD	AMBERS	CARGO
ELATE	OPAL	LARDY	AMBLE	CARP
HELP	PALE	LEAR	AMBLER	CARPS
HOAR	PALM	LEARY	AMBLERS	CARS
HOARD	PARD	LOTA	ARCH	CHAMBER
HOARY	PATE	LOTH	ARCS	CHAMBERS
HOLE	PATH	LYRATE	BAGEL	CHAR
HOTEL	PATLY	MOHEL	BAGS	CHARGE
HOTLY	POLAR	MOLA	BARE	CHARS
JALOPY	POLE	NOPAL	BARGE	CHARY
JEOPARDY	PRAT	NOTA	BARS	CHUM
LARD	PRATE	NOTAL	BEACH	CRAB
LATE	PYTHON	OLEA	BEAM	CRAG
LATELY	RAPT	OLEATE	BEAR	CRAGS
LATH	RAPTLY	PAEON	BEARS	CRAM
LATHE	RATE	PARDY	BEAU	CREAM
LAZE	RATHOLE	PATY	BEER	CREEL
LEAP	RAZE	PRAO	BEERS	EACH
LEAPT	TALE	RALE	BEERY	EARS
LEOPARD	TALON	RATEL	BEGS	EMBAR
LEOTARD	TARDY	RATH	BEIGE	EMBARGO
LOATH	TARP	RATHE	BERG	EMBARS
LOATHE	TARPON	RATO	BERGS	ERGO
LOATHLY	TOPAZ	TAEL	BLEACH	ERGS
MOAT	TYPO	THOLE	BLEAR	GABLE

GAMBLE	OGRE	AGEE	LEGERS	ARISE
GAMBLER	PIER	AGER	MABE	ARRIVAL
GAMBLERS	PIERS	AGERS	MACHREE	ARRIVE
GAME	PIGS	AGIO	MARC	AVER
GAMER	PRAM	AMBEER	MARCS	CARD
GAMERS	PREACH	AMBEERS	MARGE	CARE
GEAR	PREAMBLE	AMBERY	MERC	CARER
GEARS	PSYCH	BACH	MERCH	CARIES
GRAB	RACY	BAREGE	MERCS	CARREL
GRAM	RAGE	BARGEE	OGAM	CARRIES
HAGS	RAGS	BEMA	OGEE	CARVE
HARE	RAMBLE	CABLER	PRAHU	CARVER
HAREM	REACH	CABLERS	PRAU	CHILE
HARP	REAM	CAMBER	PREE	CHIRR
HARPS	REBEL	CAMBERS	RAGEE	CHIS
HUMBLE	REEL	CARPI	RAGI	CHIVE
HUMBLER	REGS	CHAM	RAMEE	CHOW
HUMBLERS	RHUMBA	CHARE	RHUMB	CHOWS
LEACH	SCAB	CRAMBE	SCAG	CRIES
LEER	SCAM	EERY	SCARP	DOWSE
LEERS	SCAR	EGER	SCRAG	DRIES
LEERY	SCARE	EGERS	SCRY	DRIVE
LEGACY	SCARY	GAMB	SPIEGEL	DRIVEL
LEGS	SCHMEAR	GAMBE	SPIER	DRIVER
MACH	SCRAM	GARS	SPRAG	ELVISH
MACS	SCRAMBLE	GAUM	UMBEL	EVIL
MAGE	SCREAM	GERAH	**BASIC BLOX #11**	HIES
MAGI	SCREE	GIPS	COMMON WORDS	HIRE
MAGPIE	SPIEL	GIPSY	ACRE	HIRER
MAGS	SPIELER	GREBE	AERIE	HIVE
MARCH	SPREE	GREE	AERIES	HOWS
MARE	SPRY	HAEM	ALIVE	LAVE
MARS	UMBER	HAME	ARCH	LAVER
MEGA	UMBERS	LEAR	ARCHIVAL	LAVISH
MEGS	UNCOMMON WORDS	LEARS	ARCHIVE	LEVIES
MERCY	ABELE	LEARY	ARCHRIVAL	LIES
MERGE	AERY	LEGER	AREA	LIEU

245

ANSWERS

LIEUS
LIRA
LIRE
LIVE
LIVER
LUSH
RARE
REAL
RELIES
RELISH
REVALUE
REVALUES
REVISE
REVUE
REVUES
RILE
RISE
RIVAL
RIVE
RIVER
SHIRE
SHIRR
SHIV
SHIVA
SHIVER
SHOD
SHOW
SHRIVE
SHRIVEL
SILVER
SIRE
SWIVEL
VALE
VALISE
VALUE
VALUES
VEAL

VIES
VILE
VILER
VISE
WHILE
WHIR
WHIRR
WILE
WIRE
WIRER
WISE
WISH

ARCHIL
AREAL
ARIL
ARRIS
ARVAL
CARR
CARVEL
CHIRRE
CHOWSE
CRIS
DHOW
DHOWS
DOWIE
DOWS
ERVIL
HILA
HILUS
ILEA
IRREAL
LEVA
LEVIS
LIVRE
LUES
OWSE

RACHIS
REALISE
RERISE
SHIVE
SHRI
SHRIVER
SILVA
SILVAE
SIRRA
SIVER
SWIVE
ULVA
UVEA
UVEAL
VELA
VERA
WIRRA
WIVE
WIVER

BASIC BLOX #12

AERIAL
ALEE
ALIT
ALTER
ATELIER
ATTIRE
EATER
ELATE
ELATER
ELITE
GREAT
GRIT
HAIL
HAIR
HALE
HALITE

HALT
HALTER
HATE
HATER
HEAT
HEIR
HIATAL
HILT
HIRE
LAIR
LATE
LATER
LATTE
LETTER
LIRE
LITE
LITER
RETAIL
RETALIATE
RETILE
RHEA
RIAL
RILE
RITE
TAIL
TALE
TATER
TEAT
TEETER
TIER
TILE
TIRE
WHALE
WHAT
WHEAT
WHET
WHILE

WHIR
WHIT
WHITE
WHITER
WRIT
WRITE

EELIER
GHAT
HEIL
HILA
ILEA
LATI
LEET
LIER
REATA
RETE
RETIA
RETIAL
RIATA
TAEL
TAHR
TALI
TATE
TEEL
TELA
TELE
TELIA

BASIC BLOX #13

ACES
ACHE
ACHES
ACQUIRE
ACQUIRER
ACRE
AIRER

ARISE
AURICLE
CIRRUS
CLERK
CRIER
CRISP
ESQUIRE
HACK
HACKLE
HECK
HECKLE
HECKLER
ICES
LEIS
PECK
PERCH
PERCHES
PERK
PERUSE
PRICE
PRICES
PRICK
PRICKLE
PRIER
PRISE
QUARREL
QUICHE
QUICHES
QUICK
QUIRE
QUIRK
RAISE
REPRICE
REPRICES
REPRISE
RICE
RICES

RICH
RICHES
RISE
RUSE
SICK
SICKLE
SIERRA
SIRE
SPEC
SPECIE
SPECK
SPECKLE
SQUARE
SQUARER
SQUIRE
SQUIRREL
SURE
SURER
UREIC
URIC

ACEQUIA
AREIC
ARIEL
ARRIS
AUREI
AURIC
AURIS
CEPS
CESURA
CIRE
CRIS
ERICA
HACKLER
KRIS
PECH
PEISE

PERI
PERIS
QUAI
QUAICH
QUAICHES
QUAIS
QUARE
RAIS
REIS
RERAISE
RERISE
RICK
RIEL
SICE
SIRRA
SURA

BASIC BLOX #14

ABLE
ALBUM
ALEC
ALOE
AMBLE
AMUCK
BALE
BAMBOO
BAMBOOZLE
BEAM
BLAB
BLAM
BLOB
BLOC
BLOCK
BOLO
BOZO
BUCK
BUCKO

BUMBLE
BUMP
BURB
BURBLE
CLAM
CLAMP
CLAP
CLOAK
CLOCK
COBB
COBBLE
COLA
COOK
COOL
CRUMB
CRUMBLE
CUBE
CURB
KAZOO
KOLA
LAMB
LAMP
LEAP
LOBE
LOCK
LOOK
MALE
MUCK
OLEO
PALE
PALOOKA
RUBBLE
RUBE
RUBEOLA
RUBLE
RUMBA
RUMBLE

RUMP

AMBO
AZOLE
BALBOA
BECLOAK
BLAE
BLEB
BOCK
BOLA
BOLE
BRUMAL
BUBAL
BUBALE
BUBO
COBLE
COLE
COLZA
CRUMP
KOLO
LOCUM
MABE
OLEA
RUBEL
RUCK
UMBEL
UMBO
ZOEA
ZOEAL

BASIC BLOX #15

ACNE
ALEC
ALUM
ALUMS
AMICUS
AMPULE

ANSWERS

CAFE	IMPACT	PLUS	MACLE	LOONY
CALF	IMPALE	PUCE	MACULE	LOTUS
CAMP	IMPUGN	PULP	MULCT	LOUT
CAMPUS	LACE	PUMA	PAMS	LOUTS
CAMPY	LAMP	PUMICE	PATY	NUTS
CAMS	LAMS	SIGN	PLAT	OATS
CAUL	LEFT	SIMP	PLATY	ONTO
CENT	LEFTY	SMUG	PULA	ONUS
CLAM	LENT	SULFA	PULE	OURS
CLAMP	LUCENT	SUMAC	SICE	OUST
CLAMS	LUMP	SUMP	SIMA	OUTDO
CLAP	LUMPY	TACT	SMALT	OUTS
CLAY	MACE	TALC	SULCI	ROUST
CLEF	MALE	TALCUM	TACE	ROUT
CLEFT	MALT	TALCUMS	TALUS	ROUTS
CLUMP	MALTY	TALE	TAMIS	RUNT
CLUMPY	MAUL	TALENT	TYPAL	RUST
CULT	MICA	TAMP	BASIC BLOX# I6	RUTS
ECLAT	MICE	TAMS	COMMON WORDS	STAY
ENCAMP	MULE	TAUS	AHOY	STONY
ENGULF	MUSIC	YAMS	AUNT	STOUT
FACE	MUSICAL	UNCOMMON WORDS	AUTO	STRUT
FACT	MUSICALE	ALEF	DOLT	STUN
FACULTY	PACE	AMICE	DOUR	STUNT
FAULT	PACT	AMIS	HATS	TAUNT
FAULTY	PALE	AMPUL	HAUNT	TAUS
FECAL	PALP	AMUS	HOLD	TAUT
FELT	PELF	CELT	HOLDOUT	TOLD
FLAP	PELT	CLAPT	HOLDOUTS	TONY
FLAT	PENT	ECUS	HONOUR	TOON
FLAY	PLACE	FECULA	HONOURS	TORS
FLUS	PLATYPUS	FLAM	HOOT	TORT
GIMP	PLAY	FLAMS	HOOTS	TORTS
GIMPY	PLUG	FLUMP	HOTS	TORUS
GULF	PLUM	LUCE	HOUR	TOTS
GULP	PLUMP	LUMA	HOURS	TOUR
GUMS	PLUMS	LUMS	LOON	TOURS

TOUT	TAUON	LIMP	LIPIN	BOWER
TOUTS	TONUS	LIMPING	LUNE	BOWERY
TROD	TORTA	LINE	LUNGI	BOWL
TROT	TOYO	LUMP	LUPIN	BOWLER
TROUT	TOYON	LUMPING	MULING	BROTH
TROUTS	YOUS	LUNG	MUNI	BROTHEL
TRUST	**BASIC BLOX# 17**	LUNGE	NEIF	BROTHER
TUTOR	COMMON WORDS	LUPINE	PIBAL	BROTHY
TUTORS	ABUZZ	MUZZLING	PILI	BROW
TUTS	ALBUM	MUZZY	PULA	CHEER
UNTO	ALIEN	PILING	PULI	CHEERY
UNTOLD	ALIGN	PINE	PULING	CHEW
UNTROD	ALINE	PING	PUNG	CHEWY
YAHOO	ALUM	PIZZA	ZAZEN	ELBOW
YOUR	BALING	PUZZLING	ZEIN	FEEL
YOURS	BLAZE	UMPING	**BASIC BLOX #18**	FELL
UNCOMMON WORDS	BLAZING	UNIFY	COMMON WORDS	FELLOW
ATONY	BLIMP	ZINE	BEEF	FLEE
DORS	BLIP	ZING	BEER	FLEW
HAUT	BLUING	UNCOMMON WORDS	BEERY	FLOE
HOLT	BUMP	ALIF	BELL	FLOG
HOTROD	BUMPING	AZINE	BELLOW	FLOW
HOYA	BUZZ	BLIN	BELLOWER	FLOWER
LOUR	FEIGN	BLUNGE	BELOW	FLOWERY
LOURS	FINE	BUNG	BLEW	GLOB
NOLO	FIZZ	FEZZY	BLOG	GLOBE
NOTA	FIZZY	FILA	BLOT	GLOW
NOUS	IMPINGE	FILUM	BLOTCH	GLOWER
OOTS	JAZZ	GENIP	BLOTCHY	GOBY
ORTS	JAZZING	GENU	BLOW	GOER
ROTL	JAZZY	GIEN	BLOWER	GOLF
ROTO	LABIUM	ILIUM	BOLL	GOLFER
STOA	LAZE	IMPI	BOTCH	GOTH
STOT	LAZING	IMPING	BOTCHER	GROW
STOUR	LAZY	LIEF	BOTH	GROWER
STRUNT	LIEN	LING	BOTHER	GROWL
STURT	LIFE	LINUM	BOWEL	GROWLER

ANSWERS

HEEL
HELL
HELLO
HERE
LEER
LEERY
LOBE
LOWER
OBEY
OTHER
REEF
REEL
REFLOW
ROBE
ROLE
ROLL
ROLLER
ROWER
THEE
THERE
THEY
TOLL
TOWEL
TOWER
TROLL
TROLLER
TROLLEY
TROWEL
TROWELER
WEBLOG
WELL
WERE
WEREWOLF
WOLF
WORT
WORTH
WORTHY

YELL
YELLOW
YELLOWER
BELLWORT
BOLE
BORT
BOTCHERY
BOTCHY
BOTHY
BYRE
BYRL
EERY
EYRE
FEEB
FELLOE
FELWORT
FERE
FLEER
FLEY
GROT
HELO
HELOT
HERL
LOTH
LOWE
LOWERY
ORBY
REFLEW
ROBLE
ROLF
ROLFER
ROTCH
ROTCHE
ROWEL
THEELOL
THEW

THEWY
TOBY
TOLE
TOLLER
TOWERY
TROG
TROW
WEEL
WEER
WOLFER
BASIC BLOX #19
BUTS
CITE
JEJUNE
JEST
JUICE
JUJITSU
JUJU
JUJUBE
JUST
JUSTICE
JUTE
JUTS
NEST
NUTS
PURSE
PURSUE
RUES
RUSE
RUST
RUSTIC
SPUR
STUB
STUN
TICS
TUBE

TUNE
TUNES
TUNEUP
TUNEUPS
USURP
BUTE
ETIC
ETUI
ICTUS
JUBE
JUJUTSU
NEUSTIC
PTUI
PURS
SPRUE
SPUE
URPS
BASIC BLOX #20
ABOUT
ABUT
ABUTS
ASHY
ATTABOY
AUTO
BATH
BATHS
BATS
BAYOU
BAYS
BOAT
BOATS
BOTH
BOTS
BOUT
BOUTS

BOYS
BUOY
BUOYS
BUTCH
BUTS
BUTT
BUTTS
CHAT
CHATS
CHATTY
CHUB
COAT
COATS
COTS
COUTH
CUTS
HASH
HAST
HASTY
HATH
HATS
HUTS
OATH
OATHS
OATS
OUCH
OUTS
OUTSAT
OUTSTAY
OUTSTAYS
STAB
STAT
STAY
STAYS
STOAT
STOATS
STOUT

STOUTS	STAW	HASTIER	RETIES	ATES
STOW	STOA	HATE	RUER	BAHT
STUB	STOB	HATER	RUMP	BAHTS
TASTY	STOT	HATES	SATE	BAPTISE
TATS	STOTS	HATS	SEIZE	BAST
TATTY	STOTT	HERE	SEIZER	EPHA
TAUT	STOTTS	ITEM	SEIZURE	EPHAS
THAT	TABU	MERE	SITE	ESTER
TOTS	TAUTS	METE	SIZE	ETAPE
TOUCH	TUTTY	METES	SIZER	HEPATIZE
TOUT	UTAS	METH	STAB	HEPATIZES
TOUTS	WATS	PAST	STAPH	HERM
TOYS	WOTS	PASTE	STEM	ISBA
TUBA	**BASIC BLOX #21**	PASTER	STEP	ITERUM
TUTS	COMMON WORDS	PASTIE	TABS	ITHER
WATT	APTER	PASTIER	TAPE	META
WATTS	ASTER	PATE	TAPER	METIS
WAYS	AZURE	PATER	TEMP	MEZE
YOUTH	BAPTIZE	PATES	TEMPER	MEZES
YOUTHS	BAPTIZER	PATH	TEMPI	MURE
UNCOMMON WORDS	BAPTIZES	PATS	TERM	PASE
BATT	BASE	PERM	THERE	PEISE
BATTS	BASTE	PETS	THERM	PERE
BATTU	BASTER	PHASE	TIER	PEREIA
BOTA	BATE	PHAT	TIES	PIETA
BOTAS	BATES	PIER	ZEST	PIETAS
BOTHY	BATH	PIES	ZESTER	PISTE
BOTT	BATHE	PITA	ZESTIER	PREZES
BOTTS	BATHER	PITAS	ZETA	REIS
BUTTY	BATS	PITH	ZETAS	RETE
COTTA	EITHER	PITS	ZITHER	RETIA
COTTAS	EMPHASIZE	PREZ	ZITS	RETS
COUTHS	EMPTIES	REHAB	UNCOMMON WORDS	SATEM
COYS	ETAS	REHABS	AETHER	SATI
CUTTY	ETHER	REPAST	AITS	SETA
HAUT	HAST	RETAPE	APER	SIEUR
SAUCH	HASTE	RETIE	ASEA	SIPE

251

ANSWERS

SITH
STERE
STIPE
TAHR
TAPERER
TAPIS
TEMPEH
TEPA
TEPAS
THERME

BASIC BLOX #22

COMMON WORDS

ACHES
AROSE
AROUSE
BLUER
BLURS
BLURT
BLURTER
BLUSH
BLUSHER
BOGUS
BORER
BORES
BUREAU
CARER
CARERS
CARES
CARET
CAROB
CAROUSE
CARTE
CARTEL
CARTER
CARTERS
CHARS
CHART

CHARTER
CHARTERS
CHARTREUSE
CHEAP
CHERUB
EUCHRE
EUROS
GOBLET
GORES
GORSE
GUSHER
HACKER
HACKERS
HARES
HEARS
HEARSE
HEART
HEROS
HERTZ
LURER
LURES
LUSHER
OBTUSE
OBTUSER
OUTER
OUTRE
OUTREACH
OUTREACHES
PACKER
PACKERS
PACKET
PARER
PARERS
PARES
PARKER
PARKERS
PARSE

QUACK
QUAKE
QUAKER
QUAKERS
QUARK
QUART
QUARTER
QUARTERS
QUARTZ
RACKER
RACKERS
RACKET
RAKER
RAKERS
REACH
REACHER
REACHERS
REACHES
REARS
REHEAR
REROUTE
RESULT
RETRO
RETROS
REUSE
ROGUE
ROUSE
ROUTE
ROUTER
RUBLE
RUSHER
SHACK
SHAKE
SHAKER
SHARE
SHARER
SHARK

SHEAR
SHRUB
SHRUG
SHUCK
SHUCKER
SORER
SORTER
SOURER
SUBLET
SUBTLE
SURER
TEACH
TEACHER
TEACHERS
TEACHES
TEARS
TERSE
TRACK
TRACKER
TRACKERS
TREACHEROUS
TROUBLE
TRUER
ULTRA
USHER
ZEROS

UNCOMMON WORDS

AERUGO
AERUGOS
ARETE
ARTEL
BLUET
BORTZ
BOULE
BOURSE
BOUSE
BURET

BURSE
BUSHER
BUTLE
CARSE
CHARE
CHARES
CHARK
CHERT
ELUTE
EROSE
ERUGO
ERUGOS
GURSH
HAERES
HERES
LUTEA
ORACH
ORACHE
ORACHES
OUTERS
PAREU
PAREUS
PAROUS
QUAERE
QUAERES
QUARE
QUARTE
RACHET
RARES
REAROUSE
RERACK
REROSE
RETRACK
RETUSE
ROBLE
ROUBLE
RUGOSE

ANSWERS

SERAC
SERER
SHARKER
SOUTER
SURAH
SUTRA
URARE

BASIC BLOX #23

AIRBUS
AIRPOWER
ANVIL
ANVILS
ASININE
ASSURING
AWEING
AWING
BOARS
BORING
BOWER
BOWING
BRAIN
BRAINIER
BRAINING
BRASS
BRINE
BRING
BRINIER
BRINING
BRISS
BURSA
BURSAE
BUSING
BUSSING
EARWIG
EASING
ENGINE

ENVIOUS
EVILS
GENIE
GENII
GINNER
GNAWER
INGENIOUS
INNER
LIARS
LINING
LIRAS
LIVEN
LIVENING
LOSING
LOUSING
NAILS
NAIVE
NEARING
NEARS
OARING
OLIVE
ORANG
ORANGE
ORANGIER
OWING
PORING
POWER
POWERING
PRISS
PROWER
RAILS
RAINIER
RAINING
RANGE
RANGIER
RAWER
REARING

REARS
REASSURING
REIGN
REWIN
RIVEN
ROWAN
ROWER
ROWING
SAWING
SILOS
SINGE
SINNER
SLING
SOILS
SOLING
SOLVE
SOLVING
SOURING
SOURS
SOUSING
SUBSOIL
URINE
URSINE
USING
VINIER
VINING
VIOLS
VIRUS
WAILS
WAIVE
WANING
WEANING
WEARING
WEARS
WINNER
WRING

ANILS
ARILS
ARSINE
ASSOIL
BORANE
BORAS
BOWERING
BRAIL
BRAILS
BRANNER
BRANNIER
BRASIL
BRAWER
BRIOS
BURAN
BURAS
BURIN
EARING
ENVIRO
GNARS
LIANE
LIANG
LINGIER
LINIER
LININ
LOURING
LOURS
NAIRU
NAIRUS
NARIS
NISUS
OSSIA
OURANG
PRANG
PROAS
RANIS

RASING
RAWIN
RENIG
RENIN
REWAN
RISUS
ROWEN
RUSINE
SAINING
SANING
SANIOUS
SARIN
SAWER
SUBRING
SURAS
URAEI
URSAE
VEGIE
VENAE
VENIN
VENINE
VENIRE
VINAS
VISAING
WAIRS
WANIER
WANNER
WARING
WARSLING
WRANG

MINI BLOX PUZZLE #1

**The nine-letter word
is STARGAZER.**

ARE
AREA
ARREST

ANSWERS

ARSE
ART
ARTS
EAR
EARS
EAT
EATS
ERA
ERAS
ERG
ERR
ERRATA
ERRS
GAT
GATS
GAZE
GAZER
GAZERS
GAZES
GRAZE
GRAZER
GRAZERS
GRAZES
GREAT
GREATS
RAG
RAT
RATS
RAZE
RAZER
RAZERS
RAZES
REAR
REARS
REST
SAT
SEA

SEAR
SEAT
SERA
STAG
STAR
STARE
STARER
STARGAZE
TAG
TAR
TARS
TSAR
ZAG
ZEST

ARES
ARS
ASEA
ERRATAS
ERS
ERST
GAE
GAES
GAR
GARS
GRAT
RAS
RASE
RASER
REATA
REATAS
RES
RESAT
SER
TAE
TARE
TARES

TARRE
TARRES
TAS
TRES

The nine-letter word is MEGAHERTZ.
AGE
ATE
ETA
ETHER
GAT
GATE
GATHER
GEE
GEEZ
GEM
GET
HAG
HAT
HATE
HATER
HER
HERTZ
HET
MEET
MEG
MEGA
MET
METE
METER
METH
TAG
TEE
TEEM
THE

THEE
THREE
TREE
ZEE
ZETA
AGEE
ETH
GATER
GETA
GHAT
GHEE
META
METRE
MEZE
REE
RET
RETAG
RETE
RETEM
TAHR
TEG

The nine-letter word is FORSYTHIA.
FOIST
FOR
FORT
FORTH
FORTS
FORTY
FRO
FROTH
FRY
HIS
HISTORY

HIT
HITS
HOIST
HORSY
HOT
HOTS
IOTA
IOTAS
ITS
OFT
ROT
ROTS
SAT
SATYR
SIT
STORY
STY
THIS
TIS
TOR
TORS
TORY
TRY
TYRO
AIS
AIT
AITS
FOH
FORTIS
HIST
HORST
OHIA
OHIAS
ORS
ORT
ORTS

254

ANSWERS

ROTA
ROTAS
ROTI
ROTIS
SAITH
SATI
SITH
TAS
THIO
THO
TORSI
TROIS

MINI BLOX PUZZLE #4
The nine-letter word
is PORCUPINE.
COMMON WORDS
COP
COUP
CROP
CROUP
CUE
CUP
CUR
ECRU
EURO
INCUR
NIP
OPINE
OUNCE
OUR
PIN
PINE
PINUP
POP
POUNCE
POUR
PUCE

PUN
PUP
ROC
ROUE
RUE
RUIN
RUN
RUNE
UNCOMMON WORDS
COR
CRU
ECU
INPOUR
ORC
PIU
PUR
ROUEN
ROUP
UNCO
UPO

MINI BLOX PUZZLE #5
The nine-letter word
is HARMONICA.
COMMON WORDS
AAH
AHA
ARM
AROMA
CAM
CAMO
CAN
CAR
CARMAN
CAROM
CIAO
HAM
HARM

HARMONIC
ION
MAC
MACARONI
MAIN
MAN
MANIA
MANIAC
MANIC
MANOR
MAR
MOAN
NAH
NOR
NORM
OAR
RAH
RAIN
RAM
RAN
ROAM
ROAN
ROMAN
UNCOMMON WORDS
ACINAR
AIN
ANI
ARMONICA
CAIN
CION
HAAR
HAO
INARM
MAAR
MANO
MARA
MOA

MON
MOR
MORA
NAM
NAOI
NOM
NOMA
ORA
RAI
RAIA
RANI
ROM

MINI BLOX PUZZLE #6
The nine-letter word
is BOOMERANG.
COMMON WORDS
AEON
AERO
AGE
ANGER
ARE
BEAN
BEAR
BEG
BEGAN
BEMOAN
BONE
BONER
BONG
BOO
BOOM
BOOMER
BOOR
EAR
EBON
EON
ERA

GEAR
GEM
GNOME
MEAN
MEG
MEGA
MEN
MOAN
MOANER
MOB
MONGER
MOO
MOON
MOONER
MOOR
MOORAGE
MORE
NAG
NEAR
NOB
OAR
OMEGA
OMEN
ONE
ORANG
ORANGE
ORE
OREGANO
RAG
RAGE
RAN
RANG
RANGE
REB
REG
ROAN
ROE

255

ANSWERS

ROMEO
ROOM

AGER
ANE
BEANO
BEN
ENG
GAE
GAEN
GAN
GANE
GAR
GEN
GENOM
GNAR
MENO
MOA
MON
MOR
MORA
MORAE
NAE
NEB
NEG
NOM
NOME
NOO
OBE
OMER
ONAGER
ORA
REGNA
REM
ROM

MINI BLOX PUZZLE #7

The nine-letter word
is **MARGARINE.**

COMMON WORDS

AGAIN
AGAR
AGE
AIR
AMAIN
ENIGMA
GAIN
GAM
GARNI
GIN
GRAIN
GRAM
GRAN
GRIN
MAG
MAGE
MAGI
MAIN
MAN
MANE
MANGA
MANGE
MANIA
MAR
MARGIN
MARINA
MARINE
NAG
RAG
RAGE
RAGMAN
RAIN
RAM

RAN
RANG
RANGE
RIG
RING

UNCOMMON WORDS

AGA
AGIN
AGMA
AGRIA
AIN
AMA
ANE
ANGA
ANI
ENG
ENGRAM
GAMA
GAN
GANE
GAR
GEN
GIE
GIEN
GNAR
GRAMA
MAAR
MAIR
MARGARIN
MARGE
NAM
NEG
RAGA
RAGI
RAI
RANI
RIA

RIN

MINI BLOX PUZZLE #8

The nine-letter word
is **GEOLOGIST.**

COMMON WORDS

EGO
EGOIST
EGOS
GEL
GIG
GIGOLO
GIGOLOS
GIGS
GIST
GOO
GOOS
GOT
LEG
LEI
LEIS
LOG
LOGE
LOGS
LOO
LOOIE
LOOS
LOOT
LOOTS
LOST
LOT
LOTS
OLE
OLEO
OLEOS
SOL
SOLE
SOLO

SOOT
SOT
STOGIE
STOLE
STOOGE
STOOL
TOE
TOG
TOGS
TOO
TOOL

UNCOMMON WORDS

EGIS
GIE
GIGOT
GIGOTS
GOS
ISOLOG
LEGIST
LOTOS
OLOGIST
OOT
OOTS
SOLEI
SOTOL
TOLE

MINI BLOX PUZZLE #9

The nine-letter word
is **BRIEFCASE.**

COMMON WORDS

ACE
ACES
ACRE
ACRES
AERIE
AERIES
ARC

ARE	ERASE	FERES		LEU
ARF	ERE	FES	CLEVIS	LUES
ARISE	FRIES	FRAE	ECU	RES
ARSE	IRE	FRISE	ECUS	RUBUS
BAR	IRES	RAS	LES	SEL
BARE	RACE	RASE	LEV	SER
BARES	RACES	REI	LEVIS	SUBRULE
BARF	REC	REIS	LUCE	SUQ
BARS	REF	RES	LUCES	URB
BASE	RISE	SAB	SEI	URUS
BASER	SABRE	SAE	SEL	USQUE
BRA	SAC	SEI	VIS	**MINI BLOX PUZZLE #12**
BRACE	SARI	SER	**MINI BLOX PUZZLE #11**	**The nine-letter word**
BRACES	SEA	SERAC	**The nine-letter word**	**is JAYWALKER.**
BRAS	SEAR	SERE	**is BURLESQUE.**	COMMON WORDS
BRIE	SEC	SRI	COMMON WORDS	ALE
BRIEF	SERA	**MINI BLOX PUZZLE #10**	BRUSQUE	AWE
BRIES	SERF	**The nine-letter word**	BUR	AWL
BRIS	SIR	**is EXCLUSIVE.**	BURL	ELK
CAB	SIRE	COMMON WORDS	BUS	JAKE
CAR		ELS	LURE	JAY
CARB	ABRI	ELSE	LURES	JAYWALK
CARE	ABRIS	ELUSIVE	REUSE	KALE
CARES	ACERB	ELVES	RUB	LAKE
CARIES	ARB	EVE	RUE	LAW
CARS	ARES	EVES	RUES	LAY
CASE	ARS	EXCUSE	RULE	LEAK
CERISE	BAS	ISLE	RULES	REAL
CRAB	BRAE	LEVIES	RUSE	RELAY
CREASE	BRAES	SEC	SUB	RELY
CRIES	CARSE	SEX	SUE	WALE
EAR	CERE	SIEVE	SUER	WALK
EARS	CERES	USE	SURE	WALKER
EASE	CRIS	VEX	USE	WAY
EASIER	ERS	VIE	USER	WEAK
ERA	FER	VIES		WEAKLY
ERAS	FERE	VISE	LES	WREAK

ANSWERS

YAK
YAW
YAWL
AKELA
ALA
ALAE
ALWAY
KAE
KAY
KEA
LAKER
LEA
LEK
WALER
WALY
WEAL
WEKA
WYLE

MINI BLOX PUZZLE #13
The nine-letter word
is VEGETABLE.
ABLE
AGE
ALE
ATE
AVE
BAG
BAGEL
BALE
BAT
BATE
BEAT
BEG
BEGAT
BEGET

BELT
BLAT
BLEAT
EAT
EAVE
ELATE
ELEVATE
ETA
GAB
GABLE
GAL
GALE
GAT
GATE
GAVE
GAVEL
GEL
GELT
GET
GETABLE
LAB
LAG
LAT
LATE
LAV
LAVE
LEAVE
LEG
LEGATE
LET
TAB
TABLE
TAG
TALE
TEA
TEAL
VALE

VALET
VAT
VEAL
VEG
VEGETAL
ABELE
ALB
ALT
BAL
BEL
BLAE
BLATE
BLET
EGAL
GAE
GELATE
GETA
LEA
LEV
LEVA
TAE
TAEL
TAV
TEG
TEL
TELA
TELAE
TELE
TELEGA
VEGETE
VELA
VELATE

MINI BLOX PUZZLE #14
The nine-letter word
is FACSIMILE.

ACME
AIL
AIM
AIMS
ALE
ALMS
CALM
CALMS
CAM
CAME
CAMEL
CAMS
CILIA
ELM
ELMS
EMAIL
EMS
FACILE
FAIL
FAME
ISM
LAM
LAME
LAMS
LEI
LEIS
LIE
LIMA
LIME
MAC
MACS
MAIL
MALE
MIC
MICA
MICS

MIL
MILE
MIS
SCALE
SCAM
SIC
SIM
SIMILE
SMILE
ALME
AMI
AMIE
AMIS
CIS
EMIC
ILIA
ILIAC
LAC
LACS
LIS
MAILE
MALIC
MEL
MELIC
MILIA
SIMA

MINI BLOX PUZZLE #15
The nine-letter word
is MANIFESTO.
AMEN
AMNIO
ATE
EAST
EAT
EATS

ETA	MEN	TINE	TAE	HEATS
ETAS	MESA	TINES	TAMEIN	HER
FEAST	MET	TOE	TAS	HES
FEAT	NAME	TOES	TINEA	HET
FEATS	NAMES	UNCOMMON WORDS	TINEAS	OAR
FEN	NEAT	AMNIOTE	TOEA	OAT
FEST	NEST	AMNIOTES	TOEAS	OATER
FETA	NET	ANE	MINI BLOX PUZZLE #16	OATH
FETAS	NETS	ANES	The nine-letter word	OATHS
FIE	NIT	ANI	is ORCHESTRA.	OATS
FIESTA	NITE	ATES	COMMON WORDS	ORATE
FIN	NITES	FEM	ARC	ORATES
FINE	NITS	FES	ARCH	OTHER
FINES	SAME	FET	ARCHER	RARE
FINEST	SANE	FETS	ARCHES	RAREST
FIT	SAT	MAE	ARE	RAT
FITS	SATE	MAES	ART	RATE
INFEST	SATIN	MANITO	ARTS	RATER
INMATE	SEA	MATIN	ATE	RATES
INMATES	SEAM	META	CHEAT	RATHER
IOTA	SEAT	NAE	CHEATS	RATS
IOTAS	SET	NAM	CHEST	REAR
ITEM	STAMEN	NATES	CRATE	REST
ITS	STEAM	NEATS	CRATER	RETCH
MAN	STEIN	NEIF	CRATES	RETRO
MANE	STEM	NEMA	EAR	RHEA
MANES	TAM	NEMAS	EARTH	ROAR
MANIFEST	TAME	OES	EARTHS	ROT
MAS	TAMES	SAE	EAT	ROTE
MAST	TAN	SATEM	EATS	ROTES
MAT	TEA	SATI	ERA	ROTS
MATE	TEAM	SEI	ETA	SEA
MATES	TEAS	SEIF	ETCH	SEAR
MATS	TEN	SEITAN	HEAR	SEARCH
MEAN	TIE	SEN	HEART	SEAT
MEAT	TIES	SETA	HEARTS	SERA
MEATS	TIN	STANE	HEAT	SET

ANSWERS

SHE
SHEA
SHEAR
STAR
STARCH
STARE
TAO
TAR
TEA
TEAR
THE
TOR
TORCH
TORCHES

ARES
ATES
CHERT
CHERTS
EATH
ETH
ETHS
HEST
HETS
ORA
ORC
ORT
ORTS
RARES
RATCH
RATCHES
RATH
RATHE
RATO
RES
RESH
RET

RETS
ROTA
ROTCH
ROTCHE
ROTCHES
SER
SETA
STOA
STOAE
TAE
TARE
TARES
TARO
THRO
TORA
TORC
TRES

MINI BLOX PUZZLE #17

The nine-letter word is WOLVERINE.

EEL
EON
IRE
LEE
LEI
LIE
LIEN
LINE
LINER
LIRE
LONE
LONER
LOVE
LOVER
LOW
LOWER

NEE
NEW
NIL
NOEL
NOVEL
NOW
OLE
ONE
OVEN
OVER
OVERLIE
OWE
OWN
OWNER
REIN
RELINE
REV
REWON
RILE
VEE
VEIL
VEIN
VOLE
VOW
VOWEL
VOWER
WEE
WOE
WON
WOVE
WOVEN

ENOL
ENOW
INWOVE
LENO
LEONE

LEV
LEVO
LIER
LIN
LINO
LOWE
LOWN
OLEIN
OLEINE
REE
REI
RIEL
RIN
VOE
WEEN
WEIR
WEN
WOLVER

MINI BLOX PUZZLE #18

The nine-letter word is YESTERDAY.

ADS
AYE
AYES
DAY
DEE
DEES
DYE
DYER
DYERS
DYES
EYE
EYED
EYER
EYERS
EYES

READ
READS
READY
RED
REDS
RESET
REST
SEA
SEE
SEED
SEEDY
SEER
SET
STEAD
STEADY
STEED
STEER
TEA
TEE
TEED
TEES
TERSE
YAY
YEA
YES
YET

DEET
DEETS
DEY
DREE
DREES
DREST
EDS
ERS
ERST
ESTER

ANSWERS

REE
REES
REEST
RES
RET
RETE
RETS
SER
STEY
TED
TEDS
YESTER

The nine-letter word
is APPETIZER.
COMMON WORDS
AIR
APE
APP
APT
IRE
PAIR
PAP
PAPER
PEE
PEEP
PEER
PER
PET
PIE
PIER
PIP
PIPE
PIPER
PIPET
PIT
PREZ

PRIZE
REP
RIP
RIPE
RITE
TEE
TIE
TIER
TIP
TIPPER
TIRE
ZEE
ZIP
ZIPPER
ZIT
UNCOMMON WORDS
AIT
APER
APPRIZE
PERI
PERIAPT
PIA
PREE
REE
REI
REPP
RIA
TEPA
ZEP

The nine-letter word
is EQUIPMENT.
COMMON WORDS
EMIT
EMU
EQUINE
EQUIP

IMP
MEN
MIEN
MINE
MINT
MITE
NET
NIP
NIT
NITE
PIE
PIN
PINE
PINT
PIQUE
PIT
QUIET
QUINT
QUIP
QUIT
QUITE
TEN
TIE
TIME
TIN
TINE
TIP
UMP
UNCOMMON WORDS
NEUM
NEUME
NIM
PIQUET
PIU
QUIN
QUINTE

The nine-letter word
is ESOPHAGUS.
COMMON WORDS
AHS
ASH
GAS
GASEOUS
GASH
GUSH
GUSHES
HAG
HAGS
HAS
HES
HOE
HOES
HOP
HOSE
HUG
HUGS
HUP
OHS
OPUS
PHASE
POSE
POSH
PUG
PUGS
PUS
PUSH
PUSHES
SAG
SAGS
SHAG
SHAGS
SHE

SHES
SHOE
SHOES
SHOP
SOP
SOPH
SOPHS
SOU
SOUP
SUP
UGH
UNCOMMON WORDS
AGS
HOS
OES
OSE
OUPH
OUPHE
OUPHES
OUPHS
POH
PUGH
SHA
SOUGH
SOUGHS
SOUS
SUGH
SUGHS
UGHS
UPO

The nine-letter word
is UNIVERSAL.
COMMON WORDS
ARE
AVE
AVER

261

ANSWERS

AVERS
ERA
ERAS
INURE
IRE
LAS
LAV
LAVE
LAVER
LAVERS
NUS
RAVE
REIN
REV
RIVAL
RIVE
RUIN
RUN
SALVE
SALVER
SARI
SAVE
SAVER
SUAVE
SUAVER
SUN
SURE
URN
VAS
VEIN
VIE
VIRAL
VIRUS

ARS
AUREI
ERN

ERS
LAR
LARI
LARS
NIVAL
NURL
RAS
RAVIN
REI
RIN
SAL
SARIN
SAU
SAVIN
SRI
SURA
SURAL
URSA
VAR
VARS
VARUS
VAU
VAUS
VERA
VERSAL
VIER
VIERS
VIRL

MINI BLOX PUZZLE #23

The nine-letter word

is IGNORAMUS.

AMONG
AMUSING
AROUSING
GAIN
GAM

GARNI
GAS
GIN
MAG
MAGI
MAIN
MAN
MANOR
MAR
MAS
MOAN
MORN
MOUSING
MUON
MUS
MUSING
NAG
NOR
OAR
ORANG
RAG
RAIN
RAM
RAN
RANG
ROAM
ROAN
ROMAN
ROUSING
SAG
SANG
SARONG
SIGN
SIN
SING
SUING
SUM

SUMO
USING

AGIN
AIN
AIS
AMU
AMUS
ANI
ANIS
GAN
GAR
GAUM
GNAR
INRO
MANO
MOA
MOAS
MON
MONAS
MOR
MORA
MORAS
NAM
NOM
NOMA
NOMAS
NOUS
ONIUM
ORA
ORNIS
RAGI
RAGIS
RAI
RAIS
RAMOUS
RAMUS

RANI
RANIS
RAS
RASING
ROM
SAIN
SAU
SIGNA
SIGNOR
SIGNORA

CATEGORY BLOX #1

Signs of the Zodiac

ARIES
CANCER
CAPRICORN
GEMINI
LEO
LIBRA
PISCES
SCORPIO
VIRGO

CATEGORY BLOX #2

Fruits

APPLE
APRICOT
CHERRY
GRAPE
LEMON
LIME
MANGO
ORANGE
PAPAYA
PEACH
PEAR

MAYAPPLE

CATEGORY BLOX #3
Parts of an
Automobile
BATTERY
BRAKES
BUMPER
CARBURETOR
DOOR
HOOD
ODOMETER
TIRE
TRUNK

CATEGORY BLOX #4
U.S. Presidents
ADAMS
FORD
GARFIELD
GRANT
OBAMA
REAGAN
TAFT
TAYLOR
TRUMAN
TYLER

CATEGORY BLOX #5
Mammals
COMMON WORDS
BEAR
CAT
COW
COYOTE
FOX
GOAT
HORSE
LION
MOOSE
RACCOON

RAT
RHINOCEROS
WOLF
ZEBRA
UNCOMMON WORD
COATI

CATEGORY BLOX #6
Furniture
ARMOIRE
BAR
BENCH
CABINET
CHAIR
CHAISE
COT
CRIB
DESK
RECLINER
SOFA
TABLE

CATEGORY BLOX #7
Languages
DANISH
ESPERANTO
GERMAN
GREEK
KOREAN
MANDARIN
PERSIAN
POLISH
SPANISH

CATEGORY BLOX #8
Herbs and Spices
ANISE
BASIL
CUMIN
GINGER

MACE
MINT
NUTMEG
OREGANO
ROSEMARY
SAGE
THYME

CATEGORY BLOX #9
Shades of Red or
Pink
CARMINE
CERISE
CLARET
CORAL
CRIMSON
MAROON
SCARLET
VERMILION
WINE

CATEGORY BLOX #10
Summer Olympics
Host Cities
ATHENS
ATLANTA
BARCELONA
BERLIN
MONTREAL
PARIS
ROME

CATEGORY BLOX #11
Insects
ANT
BEE
FLEA
HORNET
LOCUST
MANTIS

MOTH
ROACH
TERMITE
WASP

CATEGORY BLOX #12
Chemical Elements
ARGON
BARIUM
BORON
COBALT
GOLD
HELIUM
IRON
NEON
PLATINUM
PLUTONIUM
TIN
URANIUM
XENON

CATEGORY BLOX #13
Best Picture Winners
AMADEUS
CHICAGO
CRASH
GANDHI
PATTON
PLATOON
TITANIC

CATEGORY BLOX #14
Garden Vegetables
BEANS
BEET
CARROT
CORN
PARSNIP
PEAS
PEPPER

RADISH
SPINACH
TURNIP

CATEGORY BLOX #15
Musical Instruments
COMMON WORDS
BONGOS
CLARINET
DRUM
FLUTE
LUTE
MARIMBA
OBOE
PIANO
SPINET
TAMBOURINE
TRIANGLE
TROMBONE
TUBA
UNCOMMON WORDS
CLARION
TABOR
TAMBOUR

CATEGORY BLOX #16
Bodies of Water
COMMON WORDS
COVE
CREEK
GULF
LAGOON
LAKE
RESERVOIR
RIVER
SEA
STRAIT
STREAM

ANSWERS

RIA

CATEGORY BLOX #17
Countries Of The World
ALGERIA
ARGENTINA
AUSTRIA
FRANCE
GERMANY
IRAN
IRAQ
ITALY
NIGER
NIGERIA
QATAR
SYRIA

CATEGORY BLOX #18
Flowers
COMMON WORDS
DAHLIA
GARDENIA
GOLDENROD
LILAC
LILY
MARIGOLD
ORCHID
PHLOX
ROSE
UNCOMMON WORD
CALLA

CATEGORY BLOX #19
Hats And Headgear
COMMON WORDS
BEANIE
BERET
BOATER

BONNET
DERBY
FEDORA
SOMBRERO
STETSON
TURBAN
UNCOMMON WORDS
MITER

CATEGORY BLOX #20
NBA Teams
CELTICS
HEAT
HORNETS
MAGIC
NETS
NUGGETS
PACERS
SPURS
SUNS

CATEGORY BLOX #21
Fish
FLOUNDER
MARLIN
PIRANHA
SALMON
SOLE
STURGEON
TROUT
TUNA

CATEGORY BLOX #22
Dances
COMMON WORDS
CANCAN
CONGA
FLAMENCO
HULA
HUSTLE

MACARENA
MAMBO
SAMBA
TANGO
UNCOMMON WORD
HAMBO

CATEGORY BLOX #23
U.S. State Capitals
AUGUSTA
AUSTIN
BOISE
BOSTON
HONOLULU
JUNEAU
LANSING
SALEM

SHAPELY BLOX #1
COMMON WORDS
AIMER
AITCH
ANTSY
ARTSY
ATRIA
CAMERA
CANST
CANTS
CAPITA
CARTS
CATER
CHARM
EMITS
FRATS
FRUIT
FRUITCAKE
HAMMER
HAREM
HAYSTACK

ITCHY
JACKET
JACKETS
JACKHAMMER
JAMMER
MAKER
MATCH
MATCHMAKER
MATER
MISTAKE
MISTAKER
MISTER
MISTERM
MITER
PACKER
PACKET
PACKETS
PANSY
PANTS
PARTS
PATSY
PICKER
PICKET
PICKETS
PIQUANT
PIRANHA
PITCH
PITCHY
QUACK
QUART
QUARTS
QUICK
QUICKER
RACKER
RACKET
RACKETS
RANTS

REMATCH
REMIT
REMITS
RICKETS
SIMMER
SNACK
SNACKER
SNARF
STACK
STACKER
STAIR
STAKE
STAMMER
STAPH
STATIC
STITCH
STRAIT
STRAITJACKET
STRAITJACKETS
STRAP
STRIA
STRIATE
STRICT
STRIP
STRUT
TACIT
TACKER
TAKER
TAMER
TAPIR
TATER
TICKER
TICKET
TICKETS
TIMER
TITIAN
TRACK

TRACKER	QUIRTS	ACETIC	KILOVOLT	UNLOAD
TRACT	QUITCH	ALCOVE	LACED	VOCAL
TRAIT	RAITA	ANTED	LADEN	VOLCANO
TRICK	RAMET	ANTIC	LATHE	VOLTA
YAMMER	RAMETS	ARTICLE	LATHED	UNCOMMON WORDS
UNCOMMON WORDS	RETACK	ATONE	LOANED	ACEDIA
ACARI	RETIA	ATONED	LOATH	ACENTRIC
AIRTS	RIANT	CADENT	LOATHE	AIRTED
ARMET	STEMMA	CADET	LOATHED	ALTHO
ARMETS	STEMMATIC	CANED	LOCAL	ANTIAR
ATRIP	STIME	CANTED	NADIR	ANTICAR
AURIC	STRICK	CANTICLE	NEATH	ANTICK
AUTIST	STRIPY	CARTE	NOVEL	ANTRA
CANTRIP	TACKET	CARTED	OCCIDENT	CANTIC
CAPITATE	TACKETS	CEDAR	OCEAN	CARIED
CHARE	TAIPAN	CITED	RACCOON	CENTRA
CHAYS	TAIPANS	CLOTH	TALCED	CENTRIC
FRACTI	TAMIS	CLOUT	TALON	CLADE
FURAN	TANSY	CLOVE	TANTRA	CLOOT
FURANS	TIPCART	COOLANT	TANTRIC	CONTO
ICKER	TIPCARTS	COOLIE	THANE	COOLTH
JACKER	TIPCAT	COUNT	THEIR	DACITE
MAIST	TIPCATS	COUTH	TICKLE	DALTON
MAKAR	TITER	COVET	TIDAL	DARIC
MATCHMAKE	TITIANS	DEACON	TIRADE	DENTICLE
MAYST	TRACTATE	DEALT	TONAL	DETICK
METIS	TRANS	DEATH	TONED	ENHALO
NAIRU	TRIAC	DECAL	TRACK	ENTIA
NARIC	TRICKER	DECANT	TRADE	HALON
NAUTCH	TRIPACK	DECATHLON	TRIAD	HANTED
PACHA	SHAPELY BLOX #2	DICKIE	TRICK	IRADE
PATRIATE	COMMON WORDS	ECLAT	TRICKLE	NOCENT
PIANS	ACCENT	ETHNOCENTRIC	TRIED	NOTAL
QUAICH	ACCIDENT	HEADCOUNT	UNLACE	ONTIC
QUANT	ACCOLADE	HONED	UNLACED	OVOLI
QUANTS	ACCOUNT	IDEAL	UNLADE	RACKLE
QUIRT	ACCOUNTANT	KILOTON	UNLADEN	RADICLE

ANSWERS

RIDENT
TACET
TELOCENTRIC
THECA
THECAL
THENAL
THETIC
TICCED
TOLAN
TOLANE
TOLUOL
TOLUOLE
TONETIC
TOOLHEAD
TRIAC
TRICKIE
TULADI
VELOCE
VOLANT
VOLANTE
VOLUTE

SHAPELY BLOX #3

COMMON WORDS

ACETYL
BIALY
BICEP
BICEPS
BILES
BLIPS
BOBCAT
BOILER
BOILERPLATE
BOILERS
CALYPSO
CAPLET
CATCH
CHAIR

CHAIRS
CHALET
CHAPS
CLAPS
CLEAT
COILER
COILERS
COMBO
COMBOS
CONSPICUOUS
CONSPIRE
ELAPSE
EUCALYPTUS
HAILER
HAILERS
HAIRS
HALCYON
LAIRS
LAPSE
LATCH
LEAPS
LETCH
LETUP
LETUPS
MOBILE
MOBILES
MOIRE
MOIRES
OCHRE
OCHRES
OILER
OILERS
PAIRS
PATCH
PATLY
PEATY
PETAL

PILES
PLACE
PLATE
PLATYPUS
PLEAT
PRICE
RELIC
RESPACE
RESPLICE
RILES
SERIAL
SHALE
SHALT
SHLEP
SHLEPS
SOUPY
SPACE
SPATE
SPECIAL
SPECIALTY
SPELT
SPICE
SPIRE
SPLAT
SPLICE
SUETY
TAILER
TAILERS
TAPIR
TAPIRS

UNCOMMON WORDS

APRES
BIACETYL
BIRLE
BIRLES
BIRSE
BOUBOU

BOUBOUS
CAPHS
CHAPLET
CIRES
CLEPT
CLYPEUS
COBIA
COBLE
COBLES
COIRS
COYPU
COYPUS
ERICA
ESPIAL
EUCALYPT
HALCYONS
HAPLY
LAPSER
LEPTA
MOBCAP
MOBCAPS
MOILER
MOILERS
OCTAL
OCTYL
OUTLEAP
OUTLEAPS
PALET
PICAL
PICEOUS
PLACET
PLAICE
PLATY
PLICA
PLICAE
PLICAL
PLICATE

PLICATELY
SERIATE
SERIATELY
SERICEOUS
SHALY
SPAIL
SPALE
SPICA
SPICAE
SPICATE
SPILE
SPUTA
TAHRS
TELCO
YCLEPT

SHAPELY BLOX #4

COMMON WORDS

ABACK
ABOIL
AIOLI
ALINE
AMINO
AMMONITE
AXIOM
BACON
BAZOOKA
BLACK
BLACKMAIL
BOOZE
CABAL
COLON
COLONIZE
COMBO
COMMA
COMMIT
COZEN
DIAMOND

266

ANSWERS

LENTIL
LIMBO
LIMIT
LINTEL
LOCAL
LOCKBOX
MAMBA
MAMBO
MAXIM
MAXIMIZE
MIDLINE
MILKMAID
MOMMA
MONTE
NONCOM
NONLOCAL
OZONE
TENON
TIMID

UNCOMMON WORDS

ABOMA
ABOON
ACOLD
AMINE
AMMINE
AMMINO
AMMONO
AMOLE
AZINE
AZOLE
BAZOO
BOLETI
COLONE
COLONI
COMAL
COMMIX
COOMB

DIABOLO
DIAMIN
DIAMINE
DIAZIN
DIAZINE
DIAZINON
DIAZO
DIAZOLE
DIOBOL
DIOBOLON
IMBALM
IMINE
IMINO
KALIMBA
LIMBA
MALINE
MAXIMIN
MAXIMITE
MILIA
MIZEN
MOONLET
NIZAM
NOMOI
NONET
OBOLE
OBOLI
OXAZINE
OZALID
ZOCALO

SHAPELY BLOX #5

COMMON WORDS

ABBEY
ABBOT
ABOUT
ABUSE
ALBUM
AUTHOR

BABES
BEGAT
BEMUSE
BLABBER
BLABBERMOUTH
BLABBY
BOAST
BOATHOUSE
BOATS
BUTTS
CYBER
CYBORG
CYMBAL
FLABBY
FLAYER
GABBER
GABBY
GABFEST
GAYER
GERMY
GROUSE
GROUT
HOBBY
HOBOES
HOBOS
HOMER
HOMEY
HOUSE
HOUSEBOAT
ICEBOAT
ICEBOATS
LABOR
LAGER
LAYER
MOATS
MOUSE
MOUTH

MUTTS
OBOES
OMEGA
REBUS
REBUT
RECITAL
REGAL
RHOMBUS
ROAST
ROBUST
ROUSE
ROUST
SOBBER
SOBER
SOUTH
TABBY
THOUS
THROAT
THROATS
THROB
TIGER
TOAST
TUBAL
TUBBY
TUBER
TUBES
TUMOR
UMBER
VERMOUTH

UNCOMMON WORDS

ABBES
ABMHO
ABOHM
ATOMY
BABUS
BALBOA
BALBOAS

BEFLAG
BOTAS
BOTTS
BOUSE
BUBAL
BUBOES
BUMBOAT
BUMBOATS
CEROUS
CYMOUS
EMBAY
FABBER
FABBEST
GEMOT
GROAT
GROATS
GYBES
MOTTS
MUTASE
OMBER
OUTHOMER
REBBE
REBBES
RECIT
RHOMB
ROBUSTA
ROTAS
ROUTH
SEBUM
STATOR
SUBER
SUTTA
TABER
TABES
TABOR
TABUS
TAUTOMER

267

ANSWERS

THROMBOSE
THROMBUS
TOMBAL
TOUSE
TSUBA
TUBBER
TYMBAL
UMBOS
VERMUTH
YABBER
YAGER

SHAPELY BLOX #6

COMMON WORDS

AITCH
AQUARIUM
ATRIUM
BOXCAR
CARTS
CHUMP
DIRTS
DITCH
GAUCHO
HOBOS
HUMPH
KUMQUAT
KUMQUATS
OXBOW
OXCART
OXCARTS
POSTCARD
QUART
QUARTS
QUARTZ
STAID
STAIR
STRIA
TRAUMA

TRIUMPH
VACUUM

UNCOMMON WORDS

AIRTS
CAIRD
CUMQUAT
CUMQUATS
DRATS
GOBOS
IKATS
KARTS
MUCHO
OSTIA
OSTIUM
RATCH
TRAIK
TRIAC
VACUA

SHAPELY BLOX #7

COMMON WORDS

ABUZZ
ARCHIPELAGO
AZALEA
CRAZE
DRAPE
DRUPE
EAGLE
GAZELLE
GAZPACHO
GLAZE
HAZARD
HAZEL
HIBACHI
HIGHWAY
HUZZA
HUZZAH
LEOPARD

PARCH
PIAZZA
PUZZLE
WHALE
WHIZZ
WIZARD

UNCOMMON WORDS

APOGEAL
APOGEIC
BRACH
BRAZA
BRAZE
BUZZWIG
CHIEL
CRAPE
EPARCH
GALEA
GAZAR
GHAZI
LAZAR
PALEA
PIAZZE

SHAPELY BLOX #8

COMMON WORDS

ABLER
ACRES
ANNAL
BALLER
BALLERS
BANZAI
BANZAIS
BLOCS
BOARS
BONANZA
BONNIE
BONNY
BORES

BRACE
BRACES
BRAISE
BWANA
CANAL
CANINE
CANNY
CARBO
CARBON
CARES
CAROB
CAROL
CIGAR
CIGARS
COARSE
COBRA
CORES
CRANIA
CRANIAL
CRANNY
CRAZY
CRONY
ENABLE
ENABLER
ENABLERS
ENABLES
ENNOBLE
ENNOBLER
ENNOBLERS
ENNOBLES
GARBANZO
GARBLE
GARBLES
GARCON
INANE
LABOR
LABORS

LORES
MEZZANINE
MEZZO
MICRO
MICRON
MISCELLANY
MISER
MOZZARELLA
NARCO
NARCS
NOBLE
NOBLER
NOBLES
OMEGA
OMICRON
RACES
RAISE
RECON
RELOAN
ROLES
SCANNABLE
SCARE
SCORE
SCROLL
UNABLE
WINEY
WINNABLE
YOGIS
ZONAL

UNCOMMON WORDS

ABLES
ACERB
ANOLE
ANOLES
ARLES
AZOLE
AZOLES

AZONAL

BALLON

BALLONNE

BLAIN

BOLES

BONACI

BONACIS

BONNE

BORACES

BORAGE

BRANNY

BRONZY

CANALLER

CANALLERS

CANNA

CANNIE

CARLE

CARLES

CARSE

CELLA

COBLE

COBLES

COLES

CONIN

CONINE

CORBAN

CORSE

ESCAR

GAOLER

GAOLERS

GOANNA

INNAGE

LABRA

LANAI

LANAIS

LAWINE

LLANO

LORAN

MEGARON

MICELL

MICELLA

MICRA

NACRE

NACRES

NARES

OLECRANAL

ORLES

RACON

RAGIS

RECOAL

ROBLE

ROBLES

SCRAG

SECONAL

SERAC

SERAI

WANEY

YOGIC

SHAPELY BLOX #9

COMMON WORDS

ACHED

ARCHED

AROUND

ATRIUM

AUDIO

AUDIT

AUDITION

AUDITOR

AUDITORIUM

BIOTA

BIRCH

BITER

CARED

CARET

CAROTID

CAROTIDS

CARTE

CARTED

CARTON

CARTS

CATER

CATION

CAUTION

CHARIOT

CHARIOTED

CHART

CHARTED

CHARTS

CHEAT

CRATE

CRATED

CREATION

CREDIT

CRIBS

CROUP

CRUST

CURATE

CURATED

CURED

CURIO

CURIUM

DEIGN

DETACH

DETRITUS

DUMBS

DUMBSTRUCK

DUMPTRUCK

DUMPTRUCKS

EDITION

EDITOR

GOITER

GORED

GUITAR

GUMPTION

HACKS

HARTS

HATED

HATER

HATRED

HATREDS

HEART

HEARTS

HERON

IDEATION

IGNORE

IGNORED

IRATE

NOTED

NOTER

NUMBS

OPIUM

ORATE

ORATED

PIRATE

PIRATED

PIROGI

PITIED

PITIER

PITON

PORCH

PORED

PORTED

PORTS

POUND

RACKS

RATED

RATIO

RATION

REACH

REIGN

RIOTED

ROUND

SIDETRACK

SIDETRACKS

SITAR

SITED

SPIDER

SPIED

SPIGOT

SPITE

SPITED

STRATI

STRIP

STRONG

STROP

STRUCK

STUCK

SUITE

SUITED

SUITER

SUITOR

TACKS

TARTS

TEACH

TIRED

TONGS

TORAH

TORCH

TORCHED

TORTS

TORUS

TRACK

TRACKS

TRACKSUIT

TREAT

ANSWERS

TRITE

TRITON

TRUCK

TRUCKS

TRUST

TUCKS

TUITION

UMPIRE

UMPIRED

ACRED

ARCUS

AROID

AROIDS

ATRIP

AUREI

BIOGS

BIRCHED

CARTOP

CHARE

CHARED

CHERT

CHERTS

CRATON

CREDS

CRITS

CUATRO

CURET

CURITE

DERAT

DIOPTRE

DIORITE

DUITS

DUNGIER

DUNGS

GOITRE

GUIRO

HARED

HERIOT

KURTA

MBIRA

MUNGO

NORITE

ORACH

ORACHE

PIETA

PIGNORA

PIROG

PONGID

PONGIDS

PONGS

PUNGS

RACHET

REDIP

REDIPS

REDTOP

RETACK

RETACKS

ROTIS

RUCHE

RUCHED

RUCKS

SIGNOR

SIGNORA

SIGNORE

SIGNORI

SPIER

STROUD

STURT

SUCRE

SURAH

SUTRA

TACHE

TARED

TAUTS

TIDERIP

TIGON

TITER

TITIS

TITRE

TOITS

TRACHEID

TRACHEIDS

TROGS

TROIS

TURION

UNGOT

URAEI

URATE

SHAPELY BLOX #10

ACOUSTIC

ASTROLOGICAL

BICOLOR

BIOLOGIC

BIOLOGICAL

BIOLOGIST

BLOTS

BOCCI

BOORS

BOOTS

CLOTS

COAST

COITUS

COLAS

COLOR

COLORS

CUTICLE

GLOBE

ICICLE

IGLOO

IMPALA

IMPALAS

LOCUS

LOCUST

LOGIC

LOGICAL

LOOTS

LOTUS

LOUTS

MIXOLOGIST

OBOIST

OUTGO

PICCOLO

PICCOLOIST

POUTS

ROBOT

ROBOTIC

ROBOTS

ROOTS

STOIC

STOICAL

STOLE

STOOL

STROBE

STUCCO

SUITOR

TOOLBOX

ALASTOR

BACULA

BALAS

BICOLORS

BOCCIS

BOGLE

BORTS

CICALA

CICALAS

CITOLE

CLOOT

CLOOTS

COALA

COALAS

COBLE

COGITO

COLOG

COPAL

CUTIS

LOGOI

LOTIC

LOUIS

OBOLE

OLOGIST

OOLOGIC

OOLOGICAL

OOLOGIST

OROLOGIST

PIBAL

PICAL

PICUL

ROBLE

ROTIS

SIGLOI

TICAL

TORSI

TROIS

SHAPELY BLOX #11

ACORN

ADORN

AGORA

ALIGN

ANGORA

ARBOR

ARBORS

ARDOR	GRAMPS	BORSCH	CAMEL	MUTUAL
ARGON	HALLO	CARBORA	CAMELS	MUTUALS
BOARD	HAWKBILL	CHADAR	CLASH	NAUSEA
BOARDS	KILOGRAM	CHADARS	CLASHES	SANDAL
BOARDWALK	LILAC	COGON	CLASS	SANDALS
BOARS	LILACS	DOBLA	CLASSMATE	SANDS
BONGO	MACRO	DOBRA	CLAUSE	SAUCE
BRADS	MADAM	DORPS	CLAWS	SAUNA
BROAD	MALIGN	GARBOARD	CLEAT	SAUNAS
BROADS	MILLIGRAM	GARBOARDS	DALES	SCAMS
BROGAN	MILLION	GARBOIL	DASHES	SEAMS
CAMPS	NARCO	KIBLA	EIGHT	SHADS
CARBO	ORANG	KIBLAH	ELAND	SHALE
CARBON	ORGAN	KILIM	ELANDS	SHALT
CARDS	PARAGON	KORMA	GESUNDHEIT	SLAWS
CARGO	PARBOIL	LIBRA	GLADS	SMELT
CAROB	PARDS	LIGAN	GLAND	STUDS
CARPS	PRODS	LOGAN	GLANDS	SWASH
CHADOR	PROGRAM	MILLBOARD	GLASS	TAMES
CHADORS	RAMPS	MILLBOARDS	GLEAM	TEAMS
CHADS	RAMROD	OBLIGOR	GLEAMS	TESLA
CHALK	RAMRODS	OBLIGORS	HANDS	THAWS
CHALKBOARD	RAPSCALLION	OBOLI	HANDSAW	TIGHT
CHALKBOARDS	ROADKILL	PARANG	HANDSET	TIGHTWAD
CHAWS	ROADS	PARDAH	LANDS	TIGHTWADS
COBRA	ROARS	PARGO	LASHES	TITHE
CORDS	SCALLION	SCALL	LAUDS	TITHES
CORGI	SCHWA	SPADO	LEGIT	TITLE
CORPS	SWAMI	**SHAPELY BLOX #12**	MACES	TITLES
CRAMP	WRAPS	COMMON WORDS	MATES	TITTLE
CRAMPS	UNCOMMON WORDS	ACMES	MESHES	TITTLES
CRAPS	ADOBO	ALECS	MUSCATEL	TUNAS
DAMPS	ARGIL	ASHES	MUSCATELS	TUSHES
GOADS	ARGOL	ATLAS	MUSCLE	TUSSLE
GORPS	BILLON	AUTUMN	MUSCLES	USUAL
GRADS	BLAWS	AWASH	MUSHES	WALES
GRAMP	BOGAN	AWEIGH	MUSSEL	WANDS

ANSWERS

WASHES
WEIGH
WEIGHS
WEIGHT
WEIGHTLESS
WETLAND
WETLANDS
WHALE
WHALES

ASCUS
CAMES
CATES
CATTIE
CATTIES
CLADS
CUSHAW
CUSHAWS
DAHLS
DAUTS
DAWTIE
DAWTIES
DHALS
DUALS
GELADA
GELADAS
GHAUT
GHAUTS
GITES
HALES
HASLET
HAWSE
LADANUM
MACLE
MACLES
MATLESS
MUSCA

MUSCAE
MUSCAT
NADAS
SADHE
SADHES
SALTIE
SALTIES
SCATT
SCUTS
SCUTUM
SELAH
SEWAN
SHAWS
SHETLAND
SHETLANDS
SHEWS
SHWAS
SWALE
SWALES
TACES
TAELS
THEWS
TUSSAH
TUSSAL
UNAUS
WADSET
WEIGELA
WEIGELAS

SHAPELY BLOX #13

AEGIS
ALOHA
ALTER
AMPLY
APOGEE
APOLOGIST
APTER

APTLY
AREOLA
ARGOT
ARGOTS
AUTOGRAPH
AUTOHARP
COMPLY
COMPOST
COMPOTE
COOER
COOPT
COOTER
COOTS
COPAY
COPTER
EGRET
ERECT
ERECTS
GOOPY
GOOSIER
GRAPE
GRAPH
GREET
HAUTE
HEIST
HELICOPTER
HERETO
HERPETOLOGIST
HOPER
HOTLY
ISOGRAPH
LAPTOP
LIEGE
LOGIC
LOGICS
LOGIER
LOGOS

LOOPY
LOOTS
LOPER
MOLTER
MOLTO
MOOLA
OPERA
OUTER
OUTGO
OUTLAY
OUTPLAY
OUTPOST
PEARL
PERGOLA
PHOTO
PHOTOCOPY
PHOTOMAP
PHOTOPLAY
POLTERGEIST
POLYP
POUTER
PRECIS
PREOP
RAPTLY
RECOPY
RECTO
RECTOS
RELIC
RELICS
RELIST
REPOT
SCOOP
SCOOT
SCOOTER
SIEGE
STOGIE
STOMP

STOOGE
STOOL
STOOP
TOOTS
TOOTSIE
TOPER
TOPMOST

APOGEIC
APOLOG
AREIC
AREPA
ARGIL
ARGOL
COLTER
COMAL
COMPLOT
COMPO
COMPOS
COMPT
COOEE
COOLY
COPAL
COPLOT
COSIE
COSIER
EPHAH
ERGOT
ERGOTS
GERAH
HECTOGRAPH
HELICOPT
HELISTOP
LEGER
LEGIST
LIGER
LOCOS

LUTEA	CRUST	STINK	DRIPT	SHAPELY BLOX #15
MOOTER	CURTAIN	STINKO	DUNAM	COMMON WORDS
MOOTS	DIRTS	STRIA	DUNITIC	ANTONYM
OLOGIST	DISTAL	STRIP	DURST	ANTONYMS
OSIER	DOMAIN	SUNDIAL	INDOW	ANTSY
PALTER	DRINK	SURTAX	INDRI	ASTER
PAREO	HOUND	TAPIR	INDRIS	ASTRONOMY
PARGE	INDUSTRIAL	TAPIRS	INDUSIA	CANER
PARGET	KNITS	TAXIS	INDUSIAL	CANNOT
PARGO	LAIRS	TRIAL	INRUN	CANNY
PARGOS	LAPIS	UNITS	INURN	CANON
PARHELIC	MANIC	UNPAID	KUDUS	CANONS
PARLE	MANICS	UNPLAIT	LAIRD	CANTER
PHOTOG	MANICURIST	UNPLAITS	LAPIN	CANTO
POMOS	MANUSCRIPT	WHODUNIT	LATINO	CANTON
POTSIE	MODUS	WHODUNITS	MANURIAL	CANTONS
POULT	MOUND	WIDOW	MANUS	CANTOR
POULTER	NONDRIP	WINDOW	MAUND	CANTOS
PRECOOL	NONPAID	WOMAN	MONIST	CANTS
RELICT	NUDIST	WOUND	MONISTIC	COMELY
RELICTS	ODIST	UNCOMMON WORDS	NIDUS	CONNER
SCOTER	OPTIC	AIDMAN	NODUS	CONNOTE
STOMA	OPTICIAN	AIRTS	PATIN	CONSORT
STOMAL	OPTICS	AMNIC	PINON	EMOTE
STOPT	PAIRS	ANURIA	PISCINA	EMOTER
TERAPH	PINKO	ATRIP	PLATS	ENTRY
TOMOGRAPH	PLAID	AURIS	SCIURID	LEMON
TOOTER	PLAIN	AURIST	SCUDI	LEMONS
TOPEE	PLAIT	CITRIN	SCUDO	LEMONY
TOPOGRAPH	PLAITS	CRISTA	TAPIS	LENTO
TOPOS	RUNIC	CRITS	UNRIP	LENTOS
SHAPELY BLOX #14	RUSTIC	CRUSTAL	UNWIT	MOANER
COMMON WORDS	SCRIP	CURIA	UNWITS	MONEY
AUDIAL	SCRIPT	CURIAL	URIAL	MONSTER
AUDIT	STAID	CURST	URSID	MONTE
AUDITS	STAIN	CURTAL		MOTEL
CITRUS	STAIR	DISCI		MOTOR

ANSWERS

MOTORWAY
MOTORWAYS
MYSTERY
NEONS
NERTS
NONSTORY
NOTER
NOWADAYS
OSTOMY
RENTS
ROAST
SMOTE
SNORE
SNORT
SONNET
SORELY
STENO
STONE
STONER
STONY
STORE
STORY
SWORE
TENON
TENONS
TONER
WASTE
WASTER
WASTREL
WONTON
WONTS
WORTS
WROTE

UNCOMMON WORDS
ANCON
ANOMY
ANONYM

ANONYMS
ANTRE
ASTONY
CONEY
CONNS
CONTE
CONTO
CONTOS
MONOS
MONOSTELY
MONTERO
MONTEROS
MOTEY
NONET
NONETS
NONYL
NOSTOC
NOWAY
NOWAYS
OENOMEL
ONERY
RONNEL
SOREL
STONEY
STOREY
STROW
TONEY
TONNE
TONNER
TROWS
WASTERY
WASTRY
WONNER
YLEMS

SHAPELY BLOX #16
COMMON WORDS
ACQUIT

AQUEOUS
BOSUN
BOUND
BOUTIQUE
BOUTIQUES
CITRUS
CRITIQUE
CRITIQUES
CRUISE
CRUISER
HERBS
MINUS
MISER
QUOIT
REBID
REBIND
REBOUND
RESIN
RESOUND
RICTUS
RISER
RUINS
SOBER
SOUND
TRIOS
TURQUOISE
UNSOBER

UNCOMMON WORDS
BOUSE
CIRQUE
CIRQUES
CRUSE
EOSIN
ICTUS
INTIS
MISBOUND
QUIRT

RESID
RESIT
SUINT
TRIOSE
TURQUOIS

SHAPELY BLOX #17
COMMON WORDS
AMPLE
AMPLY
CELLO
CELLOPHANE
CELLPHONE
CLOCK
CLONE
CLONER
COLLECT
CYCLE
CYCLO
CYCLONE
HAMLET
HOCKEY
HONER
LONER
MAPLE
PEOPLE
PHENOL
PHONE
PREOP
RECOLLECT
RECON
RECYCLE
SAMPLE
SANER
STAMP
STAPH
STAPLE
TAMPON

TELLY
UNCOMMON WORDS
COLLET
HAPLY
MAHOE
PECKY
POCKY
SAMLET
STANE
STANOL
TANREC
TELPHER

SHAPELY BLOX #18
COMMON WORDS
ALIEN
AREAS
ASHCAN
ASHEN
BEACH
BEARD
BRACE
BRAIN
BRAINCASE
BRAINCHILD
BRANCH
BRAND
BRASH
BREACH
BREAD
CADET
CADRE
CADRES
CALFS
CALICO
CARED
CARES
CARET

CARTE	HADES	BRACHS	REALS	MEDIAN
CARTED	HANDCAR	BRAES	REDAN	MEDIATE
CARTES	HANDCART	CADES	SADHE	MIDDLE
CASED	HANDER	CECAL	SALIC	MIDDLEMEN
CHALICE	HARDCASE	CEILS	SARAN	MIMED
CHARADE	HARES	CHADAR	SERAC	MIMER
CHARADES	HINDER	CHARE	SERAI	MINER
CHARD	LADER	CHARED	SERAL	MOANER
CHART	LADES	CHARES	SHEND	MOTEL
CHARTED	LASED	CHICO	TERAI	NOMINATE
CHASE	LASER	CICADAE	TRANCHE	NOMINEE
CHASED	LICHEN	DAHLS	**SHAPELY BLOX #19**	ODDMENT
CHASER	RANCH	DASHI	COMMON WORDS	PAINT
CHILD	REACH	DEASH	AIMED	PANTOMIME
CICADA	SEDAN	DHALS	AIMER	PANTOMIMED
CICADAS	SHADE	DRACENA	ANIME	POINT
COILS	SHADER	ECARTE	ANION	POMMEL
DACHA	SHARD	ECARTES	DEMEAN	PTOMAINE
DACHAS	SHARE	ECHARD	DIAMOND	REMEDIATE
DANCE	SHARED	ENCASH	DIATOM	TODDLE
DARES	SHEILA	ENCHASE	DIMMER	UNCOMMON WORDS
DEALS	SLICE	ENCHASED	DINER	AIDMEN
DETRAIN	TEACH	ENCHASER	DOMAIN	AMIDE
DRAIN	TEALS	ENDASH	DOMINATE	AMINE
EARACHE	TESLA	HADAL	DOMINEER	AMMINE
ENCASE	TRACE	HANCE	DOPAMINE	DEMENT
ENCASED	TRADE	HARED	INAPT	DIENE
ENCHILADA	TRADES	HEILS	INMATE	DIMER
ENDEAR	TRAIN	HILAR	MAIMED	DOMAINE
ENDER	TRANCE	INCASE	MAIMER	DOMINE
FLARE	TRASH	INCASED	MAINTOP	DOPANT
FLARED	TREAD	LARES	MANTEL	ELMIER
FLARES	UNCOMMON WORDS	NACHAS	MANTLE	EMEER
FLASH	ARDEB	NADAS	MAPLE	ENATE
FLASHCARD	AREAL	NARES	MEANER	ETAMIN
HACIENDA	BERDACHE	RANCE	MEANT	ETAMINE
HACIENDAS	BRACH	RASED	MEDIA	IMMANE

ANSWERS

IODIN
LEMMA
LEPTA
LEPTON
MEDIAE
MEDIANT
MEDINA
MENTA
MINAE
NEREID
NIMMED
NODDLE
NOMINA
PANIER
PANTO
POINTE
POMMEE
POMMIE
PTOMAIN
REMINT
RENTE
TAMMIE
TOMAN
TOMMED
TONDI

SHAPELY BLOX #20

COMMON WORDS

AGATE
AGATES
AGLET
AGLETS
AITCH
ANGLE
ANGLES
ATILT
ATTIC
BALES

BANGLE
BANGLES
BATES
BATTLE
BATTLES
CELESTA
CHALET
CHALETS
CHAMP
CHATTEL
CHILE
CHILES
CHIME
CHIMP
CITES
CLIMATE
CLIMATES
CLIME
ELECT
ELITE
ELITES
EMAIL
EMPHATIC
GAILY
GALES
GAMILY
GATES
GLITCH
GNATS
HALEST
HALITE
HALTS
HATES
HILTS
JETLAG
LATCH
LATELY

LATEST
LATTE
LATTES
LATTICE
LETCH
LILTS
LITTLE
MAGNATE
MAGNATES
MALES
MALICE
MALTS
MATCH
MATES
MATTE
MATTES
MILES
MITES
MITTS
NATTILY
PHIAL
PHILATELY
SELECT
SETTLE
STALAG
STALAGMITE
STALE
STALELY
TAILGATE
TAILGATES
TALES
TANGLE
TANGLES
TETCHILY
TILES
TILTS

UNCOMMON WORDS

AGAMIC
AGNATE
AGNATES
ALANG
ALATE
ALATES
AMICE
ANGLICE
ATELIC
ATLATL
BAALIM
CHITAL
GALAH
GAMIC
GLIME
HALES
HALITES
HEMAL
HEMATIC
HEMIC
LAGAN
LAICH
LITTLES
MAILE
MAILES
MALATE
MALATES
MALIC
MATTS
MICHE
MILCH
MILTS
NATES
PHATIC
SELAH
SETAL

STANG
STELA
STELAI
STELE
STELIC
TANGA
TELIA
TELIAL
TELIC
TESTA

SHAPELY BLOX #21

COMMON WORDS

ALINE
ALPINE
APORT
ARMPIT
BIPLANE
BIPOLAR
BLAME
BLAMER
BLANK
BLANKET
BLARE
BLINK
BLOOP
BRIAR
BRINE
BRINK
COLOR
COLORANT
COOLANT
CORAL
DRINK
DROOL
DROOP
EMAIL
EMPLANE

EMPLOY	TAILOR	INARM	TRINE	LEEWARD
EMPORIA	TAMER	LAIRD	TROOPIAL	LEEWARDS
ENTAIL	TAPIR	LAPIN	TROPIN	NERDS
INMATE	TEMPI	LIANE	TROPINE	OARED
LAMER	TEMPLAR	LORAN	**SHAPELY BLOX #22**	OATER
LATEN	TEMPLATE	MALINE	COMMON WORDS	OFFSET
LATKE	TEMPO	MATIN	ADHERE	OFTEN
METRO	TEMPORAL	MEROPIA	BEADS	OFTER
METROPOLITAN	TRAIL	OOLITE	BEARD	RATES
NAMER	TRAIN	OORALI	BEARDS	READS
OPALINE	TRAIT	ORLOP	BEATEN	REBEL
OPIATE	TRAMP	ORPIN	BEATER	REDATE
OPINE	TRAMPOLINE	ORPINE	BEEFS	REDATES
ORATE	TRIAL	PAROL	BERATE	REEFS
ORBIT	TRINKET	PATEN	BERATES	SATEEN
ORBITAL	TRIPART	PATIN	BERET	SATES
PAINT	TRIPLANE	PATINE	BETAS	SCOFF
PLAIN	TRITE	PILAR	BRADS	SCOFFS
PLAINT	TROOP	PINETA	BREAD	SOARED
PLAIT	UNCOMMON WORDS	PINTA	BREADS	SOFTEN
PLANE	ALBITE	POORI	COATER	SOFTER
PLANET	APLITE	PREMAN	COFFEE	SOFTWARE
PLANK	ARMET	PROLAN	COWARD	SWARD
PLANT	BINAL	PROLATE	COWARDS	SWEET
PLATE	BINATE	PROLINE	DATER	SWEETBREAD
PLATEN	BLAIN	RAMET	DATES	TRADE
PLIANT	BLATE	RAPINE	DRAWS	TREAD
PLINK	BLITE	RATINE	EATEN	TREADS
POLAR	BROCOLI	REMATE	EATER	TREBLE
POLITE	COLIN	RIANT	FETAS	TREES
PRALINE	COLORMAN	TAROC	FOCUS	TWEEN
PRANK	COPAL	TENAIL	HEADS	WADER
PRATE	COPRA	TENIA	HEARD	WARBLE
REMAIL	COPROLITE	TERAI	HEART	WARDS
REMAIN	CORBINA	TRANK	HEARTEN	WATER
REMAN	CORIA	TRAPLINE	HEATER	WATERBED
REMAP	ENTIA	TRINAL	HERDS	WATERBEDS

ANSWERS

WATERED

COMMON WORDS

TIERS
TOPER
TOPERS
TORPID
UTOPIA
WAITPERSON
WEAPON
WEAPONRY
WEAPONS

UPSET
URBAN
UNCOMMON WORD
SLURB

NITRO
NORTH
REIGN
REWON
THINE
THING
WAFER
WEIGH
WORTH

ZEBRA
ZEBRAS
UNCOMMON WORDS
ARDEB
ARETE
ARETES
ARTEL
ATWEEN
BRAWS
BREES
COATEE
COATEES
COFFS
DERAT
DERATE
DERATES
DRAWEE
DREES
OATEN
RATEL
SADHE
SAREE
SAREES
SETAE
SEWAR
SOFTA
SOWAR
SWARE
SWART
SWEER
TARED
TEFFS
WARED
WOADS

AEONS
APRON
APRONS
AUDIT
AUDITOR
AUDITORS
AUDITORY
AWAIT
DIAPER
DIAPERS
FIERY
FRUIT
FRUITFUL
FUTON
FUTONS
LAWYER
LAWYERS
LAYER
LAYERS
PAWER
PAWERS
PAYER
PAYERS
PEONS
PERSON
PIERS
PITON
PITONS
POTFUL
REPAID
REPAY
REPOS
REPOT
ROPEY
SNORE

3-D BLOX #2
COMMON WORDS
DIETS
EXILE
LEASH
LEAST
LIVID
MATTE
PIXEL
PIXIE
PLEAD
PLEAS
STEAD
TASTE
TELEX
TEXTS

UNCOMMON WORDS
DAWEN
NITRE
ROWEN
TRINE

3-D BLOX #4
COMMON WORDS
ANGRY
ANGST
BANDS
BANGS
BARGE
BELCH
GRAND
GRAPE
PANGS
PURGE
RANDS
RANGE
STATE
SYRUP
TETRA
TRULY
TRYST
YACHT
UNCOMMON WORD
PARGE

UNCOMMON WORDS
AIDFUL
ALWAY
APERS
APERY
FLUTIER
OREAD
PAEON
PAEONS
PORNS
PREAUDIT
ROPEWAY
TOPFUL
YAPON
YAPONS

UNCOMMON WORDS
MATTS
SATEM
TSADI

3-D BLOX #1
COMMON WORDS
ABHOR
AFIRE
FARES
FIRES
PULSE
RITES
SERIF
SPURT
THORN
TIRES
ULCER

3-D BLOX #3
COMMON WORDS
BEGIN
BENDY
EIGHT
FEIGN
GENIE
HINGE
INERT
INFER
IRONY
NEIGH
NIGHT

3-D BLOX #5
COMMON WORDS
AVERS
DELTA
DELTS
FEVER
FIRST
FIVER
FLEET
JOKER
JOUST
RIFLE
SKATE
STAKE
STAVE
STEED
STEEL
TAKER
WAVER
UNCOMMON WORDS
DEETS
EVITE
LEETS
VERST
WAKER

3-D BLOX #6
COMMON WORDS
CHAIN
CHAIR
CHAMP
CINCH
CYNIC
MANGY
MANIA
MANIC
MYNAH
NYMPH

PSYCH
RAMPS
RANCH
RANGY
SCHWA
SYNCH
WRING
UNCOMMON WORDS
CHANG
CYMAR
MARIA
NARIC
WHANG
WRANG

3-D BLOX #7
COMMON WORDS
ADEPT
ADOPT
ATOLL
DALLY
DEPTH
DRILL
DRILY
HOPED
LIGHT
MIGHT
NODAL
PEDAL
PETAL
RIGHT
TALLY
TEETH
THONG
THREE
UNCOMMON WORDS
HONGI
LATED

3-D BLOX #8
COMMON WORDS
BERYL
BLITZ
BYLAW
FILLY
FITLY
GIZMO
GLITZ
MEALY
MERRY
MOTIF
WALTZ
UNCOMMON WORD
LIGER

3-D BLOX #9
COMMON WORDS
ALGAE
ARENA
AVERT
GLARE
GLOVE
HIREE
INERT
INKED
KNAVE
KNEAD
KNEED
LATTE
LOVER
OVERT
ROSIN
SANER
SAVER
SAVOR
SIREN
SOLAR

THINE
THINK
TREAD
TREED
TROVE
UNCOMMON WORDS
LAREE
LARIS
LORIS
NEROL
OREAD
ROVEN
SIREE
TAROS
TRINE
VOLAR

3-D BLOX #10
COMMON WORDS
JACKS
OKAPI
PATSY
PIQUE
QUACK
QUERY
QUICK
RIOTS
UNCOMMON WORDS
ERICA
POTSY
QUIRE
QUIRT
RICKS

3-D BLOX #11
COMMON WORDS
CLEAR
DINER
EARED

ENNUI
FILET
FRAME
GUIDE
INNER
RAMEN
SWINE
TEAMS
TWINE
UNCLE
WIDEN
WIDER
WINED
UNCOMMON WORDS
AMENT
GUIDS
GWINE
INFRA
INNED
RENTE

3-D BLOX #12
COMMON WORDS
AZURE
CAPED
CAPER
CEDAR
CURED
DEPOT
LADER
OPERA
PACED
PACER
PEARL
PEDAL
PORED
RECAP
RECUR

ANSWERS

REPOT
ROPED
RURAL
SPACE
SPEAK
SPEAR
SPORE
STALK
STARE
STARK
STORE
STORK
TOPAZ
TOPED
TOPER

APEAK
AREAE
ARECA
AREPA
DERAT
STADE
STOPE
TARED

3-D BLOX #13
AGUES
ARGUE
GRAMS
GRAPH
GUESS
HORSE
MARTS
PARTS
PRATS
PROPS
PROWS

SEATS
SHOPS
SMART
STARS
STRAP
SUGAR
SWARM
TRAMS
WARMS
WORMS
WORSE

ARGUS
SWOPS
TAWIE

3-D BLOX #14
ACORN
CARTS
COHOS
CORGI
COWER
EXERT
EXIST
EXTRA
GHOST
GROWN
HEROS
NEIGH
OHING
REIGN
ROSIN
ROWER
STRAW
STREW
WARTS
WEIGH

CAREX
EXINE
EXING

3-D BLOX #15
BACON
BAKES
BLOCK
BLOCS
CAKES
CELLO
COAST
COKES
CONES
COOPS
COOTS
COPSE
ESTOP
LAKES
OASES
PLACE
SPOOK
SPOON

CONTO
SCOPS
STOOK

3-D BLOX #16
BRAID
DEARY
DEITY
DIARY
MAIDS
MAIZE
MYTHS

RAIDS
SCOWL
SHEAR
THEIR
WEARY
ZEBRA

BEAMY
BRITH

3-D BLOX #17
ABIDE
AGLOW
ALLOW
AORTA
BIDED
BIDET
BLOAT
BLOWS
BLOWY
BROAD
BROWS
DADAS
DATED
DROLL
GLOAT
GLORY
GLOWS
LOATH
OATHS
SATED
SWORD
TROLL
WORTH

DASHY
TROWS

3-D BLOX #18
AERIE
ALLOT
ALLOY
DEISM
DEMON
DREAM
DRILL
HOMED
HONED
LADEN
LEMON
LENTO
LITHO
MEDAL
MONTH
NOMAD
REAMS
SHONE
SILLY
SMELL
TIRES
TREAD
TRIED
TRILL

AMENT
MADRE
RESIT
RILLE
YLEMS

3-D BLOX #19
AIDER
AUDIT
AWAIT

BLEST
BLURT
DIMES
ELBOW
ELUDE
EMOTE
FABLE
FAULT
LEMUR
LURED
MELTS
MULES
ROMEO
RULES
STRUM
TIMES
TOMES
TORTS

UNCOMMON WORDS

ABLES
BLUME
DUROS
EROSE
MITER
MORTS

MURED
REDIA
RETIA
SORED

3-D BLOX #20

COMMON WORDS

DIVAN
DIVOT
FIRMS
FLEAS
IRONS
IRONY
IVORY
LEAPS
NADIR
NORMS
RIFLE
SPASM
STONY
STORM
STORY
TAPAS

UNCOMMON WORDS

ATONY
EYRAS

ROTAS
TORAS

3-D BLOX #21

COMMON WORDS

DROWN
FJORD
FROWN
HAUNT
JAUNT
MAJOR
MOUNT
MOUTH
NINJA
NINTH
UNIFY
UNJAM

UNCOMMON WORDS

MOTHY
ROWTH

3-D BLOX #22

COMMON WORDS

ANKHS
AVERS
BLINK
BREWS

COMER
COWER
KNAVE
KNOWS
LIVER
MONTH
MOWER
NAVEL
RELIC
REWON
SHANK
SHAVE
THANK
VILER

UNCOMMON WORDS

ANILE
HAVER
LEVIN
OMBRE
OMERS

3-D BLOX #23

COMMON WORDS

BEETS
BIPED
EQUAL

EQUIP
GLADE
GUEST
GUISE
ISLET
LADES
LAPIS
MOTEL
PEDAL
QUALM
QUEST
SEPAL
SQUAD
SQUIB
TOQUE

UNCOMMON WORDS

BLETS
SEELS
SIPED
TOGUE

THE LAST PAGE

Fellow Bathroom Readers:

The fight for good bathroom reading should never be taken loosely—we must do our duty and sit firmly for what we believe in, even while the rest of the world is taking potshots at us.

We'll be brief. Now that we've proven we're not simply a flush-in-the-pan, we invite you to take the plunge: Sit Down and Be Counted! Log on to *www.bathroomreader.com* and earn a permanent spot on the BRI honor roll! No join-up fees, monthly minimums or maximums, organized dance parties, quilting bees, solicitors, annoying phone calls (we only have one phone line), spam—or any other canned meat product—to worry about...just the chance to get our fabulous irregular newsletter and discounts on Bathroom Reader products.

You can also email us:

mail@bathroomreader.com

Well, we're out of space, and when you've gotta go, you've gotta go. Tanks for all your support. Hope to hear from you soon. Meanwhile, remember...Go with the flow!

—Uncle John and the BRI Staff